SNOW GLOBES

SNOW GLOBES

THE COLLECTOR'S GUIDE TO SELECTING, DISPLAYING, AND RESTORING SNOW GLOBES

Connie A. Moore & Harry L. Rinker

KNICKERBOCKER PRESS

Published by Knickerbocker Press
276 Fifth Avenue
New York, New York 10001

This edition produced for sale in the U.S.A., its
territories and dependencies only.

ISBN 1-57715-077-5
This edition printed 1999

A QUINTET BOOK

This book was designed and produced by
Quintet Publishing Limited
6 Blundell Street
London N7 9BH

Creative Director: Richard Dewing
Designer: Peter Laws
Project Editor: Katie Preston
Editor: Maggi McCormick
Photographer: Harry Rinker Jr.

Typeset in Great Britain by
Central Southern Typesetters, Eastbourne
Manufactured in Singapore by
Eray Scan Pte Ltd
Printed in Singapore by
Star Standard Industries Pte Ltd

CONTENTS

INTRODUCTION

TOP
Hand-painted, injection-molded chimney with a snow globe in front. The rectangular-shaped globe has two molded panels and is outlined in white plastic. Children in Christmas clothing sit atop a fireplace with holly beneath their feet. Base marked "V 357/Made in Hong Kong." 1980s. 3⅛ in × 1 in × 4⅜ in (8 × 2.5 × 11 cm).

LEFT
Hand-painted bisque figure of a standing skier. Glass dome, Bakelite base, white snow. Base marked "Made in U.S.A./U.S. Patent/logo (SB Co.)/7/5282." Maker unknown. 1939–40. 4³/₁₆ in (10.5 cm). (Restored).

ABOVE

Bisque model of the U.S. Capitol. Glass ball, brown glazed ceramic base, white snow. Maker unknown. Late 1930s. 4⅛ in (10.4 cm) high. (Restored).

ABOVE

St. Louis, Missouri, souvenir molded panels. Clear plastic dome and white oval base. Back of dome painted blue, white snow. Base marked "No. 354S/ Made in Hong Kong." Late 1960s/ early 1970s. 4¼ in (10.75 cm) wide, 3¼ in (8.25 cm) high.

When you ask snow globe collectors to recall the first snow globe they remember, few can identify a specific snow globe or when they saw it. Most collectors twist the question around until it becomes: "Can you tell me about the first snow globe that you acquired after you made the decision to collect?" Then the story flows automatically.

There are valid reasons for not remembering this first "snow globe encounter." It probably happened when the collector was a young child. The first snow globe that they saw was picked up and shaken out of curiosity. Fascinated by the snowstorm that this generated, they most likely shook it again and again. Eventually they tired of this novelty, put it down, and went on to something else. The experience was momentary – instant gratification. Yet, a snow globe's spontaneity is one of its most enduring qualities. Except in a few instances, snow globes have no utilitarian purpose. Their role is to bring pleasure.

Children acquire their first snow globes as gifts or souvenirs. When received, they are displayed in a place of honor on a shelf or table. However, within a short time their attraction fades, and they are relegated to drawers, closets, or other hidden storage places. As the child matures and leaves home, the snow globes are discarded as childish objects that have no place in the adult world. Fortunately, more and more adults are rediscovering their childhoods and childhood treasures.

Older snow globes became collectible in the late 1970s and early 1980s. One positive aspect of the 1980s kitsch collecting craze was recognition that there was joy in collecting the ridiculous as well as the sublime. Actually, 1980s kitsch collectors were hardly pioneers. The Victorians fully recognized the value of kitsch collectibles as did middle-class adults of the 1950s, the group responsible for assembling the first figural salt and pepper shaker collections. It is no small coincidence that the first of these eras launched the snow globe as a form and the second marked the golden age of the plastic snow globes.

Until the early 1980s snow globe collectors were largely closet cases. They existed, but kept quietly to themselves. Select friends knew about their addiction. No one talked about it publicly for fear of embarrassment. On rare occasions a snow globe collector would meet another snow globe enthusiast at a flea market or garage sale. Names were exchanged, and correspondence begun. An underground collectors' network existed.

LEFT
**Enesco Santa's Mail Waterball
from the M. Gilmore Collection.
Clear plastic dome and red round
base with letters to constitute
snow. Made in China,
copyrighted 1989. 4½ in (11.5 cm).**

ABOVE
**Combination snow globe and
ring-toss game. The object is to
get the rings onto the neck of the
flamingo. Clear plastic bullet-
shaped dome and white round-
footed base, white snow. Bottom
has applied label for
"Snowdomes/Abbeville Press,"
handed out as promotional
giveaway at the 1990 American
Booksellers Association
convention. 3 in (7.6 cm) high.**

In the mid 1980s, two key events, the arrival of Nancy
McMichael on the scene and the increasing popularity of mail-
order catalog sales, changed the course of snow globe collecting.

There are numerous instances in the history of antiques and
collectibles where one individual shaped and unified a collecting
category. Nancy McMichael of Washington, D.C., is one such
individual. Almost single-handed, she has put snow globe
collectors from around the world in touch with each other and
created a research foundation upon which others can build.

Nancy is one of those unique collectors who asked all the right
questions: what is the history of my favorite objects; who made
them; how were they made; when were they made; how were they
marketed; why did they survive; who saves them; and, how many
others like me are there? Her initial search revealed that very little
information existed in traditional sources about snow globes. If she
wanted to learn about snow globes, she would have to research
them herself. She did.

Nancy's research initiatives took several forms. She ran
advertisements in collector papers to identify and open lines of
communication with other collectors. Nancy then established
contact with snow globe manufacturers, recorded their history, and
started to research the history of those manufacturers no longer in

business. She went on to publish her research in a series of articles
in trade papers, requesting individuals with more information to
contact her so that she could share it with others.

In 1990 Nancy organized a snow globe collectors' club. In
addition to sponsoring an annual meeting, the club issues a
quarterly newsletter, *Snow Biz*. *Snow Biz* contains articles about
snow globe history, contemporary manufacturers and designers,
care, and restoration. Collectors actively participate in the
classified section, which serves as one of the principal vehicles for
trading and selling snow globes. Advertisements appear from
individuals around the world. Annual membership is $10.00
(U.S.). You can send a check for a year's membership to *Snow Biz*,
PO Box 53262, Washington, D.C.

As more and more new snow globes appear – from a variety of
sources such as giftware distributors, mail order catalogs, and
museums – they reawaken interest in older snow globes among a
broad spectrum of collectors. A twenty- or thirty-year-old collector
views a snow globe from the 1950s as old. With a minimum of
effort, collectors are quickly able to assemble collections
numbering hundreds of pieces at an average cost less than $5.00
per item. Common snow globes from the 1950s and later are found
with a minimum of effort and time at prices under two dollars.

Affordability and fun are the two ingredients fueling the current
snow globe collecting market. As long as they remain dominant,
and older examples are less expensive than contemporary ones,
the number of collectors will continue to grow. The future looks
bright for snow globe enthusiasts.

However, there are a few danger signs on the horizon. Within
the past two years, prices for pre-1940 snow globes have risen.
Many themes cross over into other collecting categories. Snow
globes have attracted crossover collectors who now compete
actively and are often willing to pay far higher prices than snow
globe collectors. A Driss Company Lone Ranger snow globe is far
more valuable to a Lone Ranger collector than to a general snow
globe collector. The recent western home decorating craze has
driven up the price of western theme examples.

Despite the trend of higher prices for older snow globes, the
pure fun inherent in snow globe collecting remains strong.
Collectors no longer hide. Instead, they openly and proudly
display their treasures, immune to criticisim from outsiders. Snow
globes are most definitely "in."

— CHAPTER ONE —

WHAT IS

A SNOW GLOBE?

TOP

**Philadelphia souvenir snow globe
showing Liberty Bell and Betsy
Ross, plus Independence Hall and
the Betsy Ross house. Clear
plastic dome and white oval-
footed base, white snow. Base
marked "Made in Hong Kong/
No. B." 1960s. 3 in (7.6 cm) high.**

LEFT

**Hand-painted bisque figure of a
snow baby ice skating. Glass
dome, brown glazed ceramic
base, white snow. Maker
unknown. Late 1930s. 4⅛ in
(10.4 cm) high. (Restored).**

Hand-painted bisque figure of a lighthouse keeper's house and lighthouse. Glass dome, Bakelite base, white snow. Base marked "Made in U.S.A./U.S. Patent/logo (SB Co.)/7/5282." Maker unknown. 1939–40. 4³/₁₆ in (10.5 cm) high. (Restored).

Snow globes are glass or plastic containers that are filled with liquid, have as their central focus a figure or panel scene, and, when picked up and shaken, produce a snowstorm that all but obscures the figure or panel. Chances are that you have caused hundreds of these miniature snowstorms yourself. Seeing a snow globe sitting idle is a temptation almost impossible to resist.

What is the correct name for this fascinating object? Is it snow globe, snow dome, water globe, or something else? In order to collect effectively, collectors need a common descriptive vocabulary. Exchange of information, trading, or selling is difficult if confusion exists.

Snow globe collecting is a category where the creation of a collecting vocabulary became the responsibility of those individuals who did the initial research and writing. Ideally any collecting vocabulary should conform to that used by the manufacturers and distributors who create and sell the product. Alas, no universal vocabulary exists, and standard references are of little help. Neither *Webster's Ninth New Collegiate Dictionary* published by Merriam-Webster, Inc., of Springfield, Massachusetts nor *Webster's New World Dictionary of the American Language, Second College Edition* published by William Collins Publishers, Inc., of Cleveland, Ohio, contain definitions for the term snow globe, snow dome, or water globe. Collectors have been left on their own.

Box for a Souvenir Salt and Pepper Set, NO. 1372A. Made in Hong Kong. Box measures 3⅜ in × 2⅜ in × 2½ in (8.5 × 6 × 6.3 cm).

ABOVE
Turtle Back Zoo near West Orange, New Jersey. Three injection-molded panels (a turtle; a deer, leopard, and zebra; a zoo entrance). The bottle is square shaped. Back of bottle painted blue, silver flitter. End panel of bottle marked "Made in Hong Kong." 1970s. 6½ in (16.5 cm) wide, 2¾ in (7 cm) high.

The first collectors were faced with an overwhelming number of choices: blizzard-weight, crystal-shakes, schneekugel (snow ball), snow dome, snowfall weight, snow globe, snowscene, snowshakes, snowstorm, water ball, water globe, water-filled (paper)weights, and more. None of these terms fits every applicable case.

In the Victorian era, English writers referred to the novelties as snowstorms, a term that remains prevalent among English distributors and collectors. The principal difficulty with the use of "snowstorm" is that it is easily confused with a weather condition.

Many modern manufacturers use the term water globe, especially for globes imported from Austria and Germany. Besides the fact that many of the shapes are no longer globular, the term simply lacks pizzazz. It has found no favor among collectors.

Both snow dome and snow globe imply a specific shape. In truth, one finds snow scenes in an endless variety of shapes — bottle, cube, drum, and rectangle among the more common. It is possible to buy a set of drinking glasses that produce a snowstorm when the glass is tilted.

In contemporary snow globes even the term "snow" is questionable. Many modern snow globes utilize a variety of geometric shapes and materials. At best, "snow" is a generic term that describes the material that clouds the interior. The correct technical term for snow is *flitter*.

Since no term adequately describes every single object in this collecting category, a generic term must be selected. As a tribute to the earliest forms and its widespread recognition among collectors, snow globe has been chosen as the term throughout the book.

SNOW GLOBE PATENTS

Snow globe designers and manufacturers frequently patented their ideas. As a result, information about materials used, method of assembly, and manufacturing techniques that would otherwise have been lost is readily available. In addition to helping snow globe scholars, this information is invaluable to individuals restoring old snow globes.

Four principal American patents have been located. Joseph Garaja of Pittsburgh, Pennsylvania, received Patent 1,741,692 on December 31, 1929. William M. Snyder was granted Patent 2,361,43, 2,361,424, and 2,361,425 on October 31, 1944. Each of the Snyder patents addresses specific problems associated with the manufacture of snow globes from achieving a fluid tight seal to a closure device that allows for the expansion and contraction of the liquid.

Additional research opportunities exist. Snow globes manufactured by SB Co. are marked "U.S. PATENT," but no number is given. The Bakelite base of a Canadian dome reads: "Patent Applied For Metropolitan Supplies Ltd. Canada Reg. 1948." American researchers do not have a copy of the registration papers for the plastic-domed snow globe filed by the German firm of Walter & Prediger.

Snow globe patents represent an important first research step to providing greater insight into the manufacture of snow globes. The next task is to locate and record the remembrances of employees and owners of snow globe factories in the period immediately prior to and after World War II.

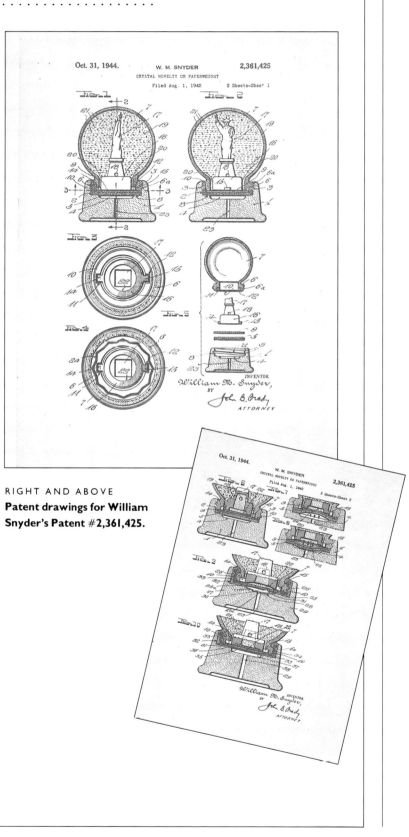

RIGHT AND ABOVE
Patent drawings for William Snyder's Patent #2,361,425.

— CHAPTER TWO —

A HISTORY

OF SNOW GLOBES

TOP

Molded three-dimensional dog, which resembles Snoopy from *Peanuts,* **pulling a sled. Clear plastic dome, white round-footed base, and white snow. Base marked "Made in Hong Kong/ No. 833." 1960s. 3⅞ in (10 cm) wide, 2¾ in (7 cm) high. With slight changes, the issue of trademark or copyright infringement may be avoided.**

LEFT

American souvenir globe using a hand-tinted photograph on plastic. Glass dome, originally oil filled with gold glitter, now has water and white snow. Plastic base marked "Made in U.S.A." Late 1930s. 4⅛ in (10.4 cm) high. (Restored).

One of the earliest mentions of snow globes occurs in the report of the United States Commissioners, headed by Richard C. McCormick, on the "Exhibition of the Works of Art and Industry of All Nations," held in Paris between May 1 and October 10, 1878. Charles Colne, the assistant secretary to the United States Commission responsible for the report on glass, noted that one exhibitor featured

> "Paperweights of hollow balls filled with water, containing a man with an umbrella. These balls also contained a white powder which, when the paperweight was turned upside down, falls in imitation of a snowstorm." (*Exposition Universelle 1878, Reports of the Commissioners.* Volume 3, page 266 *Paris.*)

Unfortunately, Colne did not identify the specific manufacturer.

Nancy McMichael has discovered that seven manufacturers exhibited "snowstorm" paperweights at the 1878 exhibition, but no company names are given. Glass makers from a number of countries, such as France and Austria-Hungary, exhibited paperweights in the 1878 exhibition, so although it is difficult to attribute the origin of the snow globe to a specific country, the concept must have been popular for some time before the exhibition.

Modern experts believe that the snow globe evolved from the solid paperweight, and a number of paperweight experts have suggested that the form was known as early as the 1840s or 1850s. Other paperweight scholars are skeptical of this early date, but we do know that the snow globe was definitely part of the 1870s lifestyle of "modern" upper-class Victorian families.

The snow globe fitted perfectly with the Victorians' love of kitsch. Any typical Victorian parlor was filled with knickknacks, some personal, some treasured souvenirs, and some simply funky. All served a primary role as conversation pieces.

Victorians traveled – to the mountains, to the shore, and abroad. Wherever they went, they brought home souvenirs as remembrances. Manufacturers quickly responded by incorporating location labels on a host of products made from every material imaginable. The glass paperweight, with a pictorial image ranging from a local scene to an advertisement for a hotel or popular tourist attraction, was one of the more popular souvenirs.

Often the Victorian parlor contained one or more glass domes resting on a round wooden base. These domes protected a variety of objects, from religious relics and groupings to hair or wax floral sculptures. Landscape and other scenes were also common.

ABOVE

Ceramic Eiffel Tower. Thin glass ball, ceramic base, dried flakes of a ceramic composition; some liquid has evaporated. Impressed under base: "L. L. Paris Made in France," *circa* **1890s. Base 1¾ × 1¾ × ⅞ in (4.5 × 4.5 × 2.25 cm), sphere 2⁹⁄₁₆ in (6.5 cm) in diameter. One of the earliest snow globes imported into the United States.**

Courtesy of the Bergstrom-Mahler Museum, Neenah, Wisconsin

RIGHT
Facade of castle and girl sailing a balloon. Clear glass dome with a square base. Half of the liquid has evaporated, and the rest has turned brown. Unknown maker. French, circa 1870–90. Base 1⅞ in (4.75 cm).

Courtesy of the Bergstrom-Mahler Museum, Neenah, Wisconsin

ABOVE
Hand-painted bisque figure of a boy on a sled with his legs in the air. Glass ball with a black ceramic base. The white snow has turned tan with age. Atlas Crystal Works. Base contains patent information and Covington, TN, location. Circa 1944–48. 4 in (10 cm) high.

In the collection of the Bergstorm-Mahler Museum in Neenah, Wisconsin, is a French snow globe featuring as its central figure the Eiffel Tower, the centerpiece of the 1889 Paris World's Fair.

From 1900 the affordable snow globe arrived upon the scene, and the snow globe became one of the souvenir forms available at tourist locations throughout Europe. Like any collectible, the snow globe enjoyed periods of popularity – the 1920s and 30s and again in the 1950s. At other times it was neglected, but as this book is being written, the snow globe is once again very much in vogue.

By the early part of the 20th century, the production of snow globes had spread throughout the European continent. Manufacturers were located in Austria, Czechoslovakia, France, the Bavarian region of Germany, and Poland. Few of these early snow globes contain a manufacturer's mark; they were most likely the products of a small-scale, cottage industry.

One manufacturer that has been trading from this early period is Erwin Perzy of Vienna, Austria. Perzy's early snow globes consisted of a glass ball resting on a tall, black pedestal base. This form dominated snow globes until after World War II. Many early Perzy snow globes have a religious theme, such as the Church of Maria Zell, a popular turn-of-the-century pilgrimage site. For more details of manufacturers, see the appendix.

Once the snow globe was established as a popular souvenir, it was never out of production. While some souvenir types featured

MODERN NOVELTY MANUFACTURING COMPANY
· ·

Pittsburgh, Pennsylvania. The 1940 and 1941 Pittsburgh telephone directories indicate that the Modern Novelty Manufacturing Company was located at the home of Joseph Garaja, 843 Spring Garden Avenue. This is obviously the same Joseph Garaja who was granted Patent No. 1,741,692 for a special design paperweight on December 31, 1929.

Garaja is not mentioned in the 1927 Pittsburgh city directory, but two novelty companies are: Novelty Manufacturing and Sales at 301 Lacock West and Novelty Supply Company at 208 Wood. Garaja obviously was involved in the manufacture of the 1929 "Novelty Pond Ornaments" based on his patent.

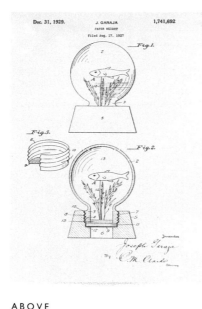

ABOVE
Patent drawing for Joseph Garaja's Patent #1,741,692.

identifiable buildings and scenes, most images were generic. In addition to religious motifs, early snow globes focused on storybook characters like Little Red Riding Hood, general representations, and sentimental and nostalgic motifs. In most cases, the information was placed on the base using a decal.

Not all early snow globes were souvenirs. Some were created as toys (just for the fun of shaking) or paperweights (temptation for temptation's sake). Some, like the snow globe with the central figure of Charles Lindbergh issued in the late 1920s to commemorate his solo flight across the Atlantic on May 21, 1927, marked special events and individuals.

Several European manufacturers, including Koziol of Erbach, Germany, began exporting snow globes to the United States in the 1920s. All these examples were of the ball variety with large pedestal bases, and cobalt blue was a favorite base color.

On August 17, 1927, Joseph Garaja of Pittsburgh, Pennsylvania, filed a patent for "an improvement in paper weights and more particularly a paper weight or desk ornament having features of artistic attractiveness and novel ornamentation." Using a piece of string secured to the stopper base of the ball, he was able to "move" a fish through a growth of sea plants. His patent, Number 1,741,692, was granted on December 31, 1929.

The Garaja paperweight patent makes no mention of the addition of snow to enhance the novelty value of the weight. However, Johnson Smith and Company, a seller of novelties by mail order, offered the Garaja patented snow globe as one of three "Novelty Pond Ornaments" in its 1929 catalog. Two globes featured moveable objects – one a fish through seaweed and the second a bird (duck or swan) through seaweed. The third contained "a miniature snowman with the snowflakes blowing all around him whenever the ornament is disturbed, until the flakes gradually settle to the bottom." This snow globe was obviously supplied by Garaja and until an earlier example is found, Garaja's snowman remains the first American-made snow globe.

Like any good idea, Garaja's concept was quickly copied. Japanese manufacturers made similar action snow globes by the early 1930s. In addition the Japanese began manufacturing and exporting large numbers of traditional snow globes in the ball format with a ceramic base. In the 1930s Modern Novelty of Pittsburgh, Pennsylvania, made snow globes with a Bakelite sloped pedestal base.

ABOVE
Two hand-painted bisque military motif snow globes. Glass domes with black ceramic bases, and white snow. Atlas Crystal Works. 1941–43. 4⅛ in (10.5 cm) high. (Restored).

In the late 1930s, SB Co., a new American company entered the snow globe picture, and produced over two dozen ball snow globes with Bakelite bases as well as a range of snow globe ashtrays. The snow globes are marked on the base "MADE IN U.S.A/U.S. PATENT/logo (initials SB Co.)/ a number 1 through 8/5282." At least four different variations of bisque central figures have been found for a single number. SB Co. ashtrays contain similar markings except that "5282" becomes "5222". The central motif in the ashtray was either a bisque figure or a hand-tinted photograph. SB Co. survived for only a short period of time – between 1939 and 1941.

As World War II loomed the snow globe enjoyed a period of increased popularity. Form variations increased as manufacturers experimented with the shape of the container and base, type of snow, and subject matter of the interior figure or scenic panel. Series were introduced as a means of boosting sales, such as a series featuring women in the native costumes of foreign lands. Even hobbyists expressed an interest in reading about and trying their hand at making snow globes.

Sales of snow globes increased threefold in 1940 when RKO Radio Pictures, Inc. released *Kitty Foyle: The Natural History of a Woman*, starring Ginger Rogers. Ginger Rogers won an Academy Award as Best Actress for her performance as Kitty. A snow globe with a bisque figure of a young girl sledding down a hill from a castle serves as the transition element between principal scenes.

While production ceased in a great many areas during World War II, snow globes were not affected. Limited production did take place. William M. Snyder's Atlas Crystal Works produced ceramic base, ball snow globes first in Trenton, New Jersey, and later in Covington, Tennessee. The company quickly became the leading American manufacturer of that type of snow globe.

Wars produce technological advances, and World War II was no exception. Tremendous strides were made in the manufacture of plastic, especially with increased sophistication in injection molding. Suddenly the plastic dome-shaped snow globe became the dominant style.

Austria, Germany, and Japan were all major pre-war exporters of snow globes, and it was the German manufacturers who recovered most quickly after the war. By 1950 German-made snow globes were offered for sale at the Nuremberg International Toy Show by two leading manufacturers: Koziol and Walter & Prediger. Both manufactured dome-shaped snowdomes, and both felt they had originated the form first. The dispute went to court and led to what has been dubbed the 1950s "snowball fight."

Bernhard Koziol, Sr., and Hans Walter were both West German pin and brooch manufacturers, specializing in city and regional souvenir pins as well as animal and scenic pins for the general market. By the 1950s both were making their pins from plastic instead of natural materials such as ivory. Finding themselves with a surplus, they each came up with the idea of using their excess supplies to provide the central motif in a snow globe.

Koziol, who had manufactured ball-shaped snow globes in the 1930s but ceased production at the beginning of World War II, was inspired when he glanced through the dome-shaped rear window of his Volkswagen at a snowy winter landscape in 1950. He created a plastic dome-shaped snow globe that featured a pin as the main motif. Since the pins were flat, they could not be viewed effectively from the back, so Koziol painted a solid color "backdrop" for the snow globe.

The competition between Koziol and Walter & Prediger was fierce. In 1954 the issue of who had the right to manufacture domed-shaped snowdomes was debated in a German court. While Koziol's story had charm, the company lost. Hans Walter had filed the required Registration papers first. Walter & Prediger received the exclusive right to manufacture dome-shaped snow globes in

ABOVE
Hand-painted, injection-molded figure of a Royal Canadian Mounted Policeman. The horse moves on a track. Plastic dome, footed, white snow. Made in Hong Kong, marked L 635. *Circa* **1950s. 2¼ in (5.7 cm) high.**

ABOVE
Five hand-painted injection-molded units. Bottom of white base can be removed and contains unit for two AA batteries and bulb. The light reflects up into the snow globe to light up the central image. Base of dome marked "Made in Hong Kong/414 L." 1970s. Oval base – 4⅜ in × 3 in (11 × 7.6 cm), 3⅝ in (9 cm) high.

ABOVE
Three molded silhouette panels of a horse and carriage, building, and line of trees. Square plastic bottle, blue painted background, and silver glitter snow. Plastic bottom of the bottle with relief marking of "Made in Hong Kong." No date. 6¼ in (15.9 cm) wide, 2¾ in (7 cm) high.

TOP
Three molded panels – one of Rock City Gardens Inn, the other two of waterfalls. The plastic bottle has a square body with the background painted blue. Silver glitter snow. Plastic bottom of bottle with relief marking "Made in Hong Kong." Circa 1960s. 5¼ in (13.3 cm) wide. 2⅜ in (6 cm) high.

West Germany. Koziol's response was to return to the traditional bullet-shaped dome and develop a program devoted to innovation in motif and shape.

Far Eastern manufacturers, notably in Japan and Hong Kong, followed quickly on the heels of the Germans. The ball-shaped dome on a base remained the favored form, although plastic replaced glass as the material used for the balls. Whereas European snow globe manufacturers continued to use traditional figures and scenic panels, Far Eastern manufacturers proved more flexible, and an endless variety of motifs streamed across the Pacific Ocean.

Snow globes manufactured in the Far East in the 1950s and early 1960s ranged from those featuring quality construction, well-painted central motifs, and ample snow, to ones that were poorly constructed and often contained errors in spelling, attribution, and/or detail. Many designs were pirated from Europe.

A snow globe renaissance occurred in the late 1950s and 1960s. Almost every family owned one or more of these clever novelties. There seemed no limit to snow globe designs. The basic shape vocabulary expanded. Mechanical action was added to make things move, bob, and swing. Utilitarian snow globes, such as The Parkersmith Corporation's salt and pepper shaker snow globe set, were developed. The addition of music boxes and illumination brought the snow globe into the present.

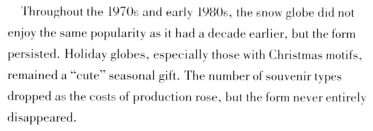

RIGHT
A souvenir from London featuring two panels (an ocean freighter, and Tower Bridge). Clear plastic dome and white oval base, back of dome painted blue, white snow. Base marked "Made in China." 1990s. 3 in (7.6 cm) high.

Throughout the 1970s and early 1980s, the snow globe did not enjoy the same popularity as it had a decade earlier, but the form persisted. Holiday globes, especially those with Christmas motifs, remained a "cute" seasonal gift. The number of souvenir types dropped as the costs of production rose, but the form never entirely disappeared.

In the mid-1980s a snow globe resurgence occurred on two levels – mail-order retailers and collectors. First, several leading giftware distributors began marketing well-made, special-focus snow globes to mail-order catalog retailers. Some were priced moderately, others were expensive. Initial sales successes created more interest, and designers were engaged to develop new motifs. Several manufacturers focused on artist and character licensing. Snow globes became an important support in specialized market areas such as Enesco's *Precious Moments*.

Strong collector interest in snow globes at flea markets and antiques shows was first evident in the mid-1980s. In 1988 the third edition of *Warman's Americana & Collectibles*, America's leading collectors' guide to twentieth-century material, included snow globes as a major collecting category. Nancy McMichael served as the Warman's advisor. Nancy's *Snowdomes* and *Snow Biz*, the newsletter for snowdome collectors, followed shortly thereafter. Snow globe collecting had come of age and was firmly established as a collecting category.

ABOVE
Paper labels around the bottles read "O'Blarney BEER." Inside each bottle is an injection-molded shamrock with white letters. The clear plastic bottles have green bottle caps and bases, and green shamrock snow. Paper labels on the bottom read "Enesco/Design Giftware/© 1989 Enesco Corporation/Designed by Mark Cook/Made in China." 4½ in (11.5 cm) high.

CHAPTER THREE

THE ANATOMY
OF A SNOW GLOBE

TOP
**Clear plastic, bullet-shaped dome
and white round-footed base, and
white snow. Base marked
"V 353/Made in Hong Kong."
Late 1980s. 3 in (7.6 cm) high.**

LEFT
**Hand-painted bisque figure of a
young girl holding an umbrella.
Glass dome, brown glazed
ceramic base, white snow. Maker
unknown. Late 1930s. 4⅛ in
(10.4 cm) high. (Restored).**

RIGHT
Mechanical, bottle-shape featuring a silhouette of a cathedral and a river ferry. The boat moves on a track in a plastic bottle with a blue painted background and white snow. Unknown maker, 1988. 5½ in (14 cm) wide.

When you dissect a snow globe, you quickly realize that its anatomy is far more complex than it first appears. Consider the following basic questions: what are its key structural parts; what liquid works best; what substance makes the best snow; and, can you have a snow globe without snow?

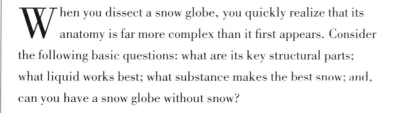

················· SHAPE ·················

Snow globes come in a variety of shapes. The two most common are the ball/globe and dome/half-oval shape. Numerous dome shape variations are known. Some have flat backs; others are elongated and described by terms such as bullets and popsicles. In the Summer 1992 *Snow Biz* Nancy McMichael began publishing shape silhouettes to assist collectors. However, a universal form chart has not been developed.

The following list classifies the nine basic forms most commonly encountered; variations are numerous.

BALL A snow globe whose primary shape is a round ball or globe sitting on a base. The ball is predominant and stands by itself. The base upon which it is set may contain other three-dimensional features, but the snow globe is always the primary design element, not a secondary one, such as a snow globe in a ball shape surrounded by a seashell collage.

BOTTLE Snow globe bottle shapes are found in the traditional ship-in-the bottle format or in the upright form of a traditional soda bottle. Round bottles meant to be viewed lying down often rest on a wooden or plastic stand. Such a snow globe is incomplete if the stand is missing.

CONICAL Snow globes that are truly conical in shape are not widely found, but are known. More easily found are snow globes

BELOW
This Scottish bagpiper appears in a clear, plastic round bottle with a green plastic base. Back of bottle painted light blue, white snow. Base marked "Made in Hong Kong." 1960s/70s. 5½ in (14 cm) high.

ABOVE

A bullet-shaped clear plastic dome and round white footed base, white snow. Base marked "Made in China/353." Late 1980s. 3 in (7.6 cm) high.

ABOVE

Clear plastic cone with a round black base and white snow. Base marked "Made in Hong Kong/No 1420." 1980s. 4¼ in (10.75 cm) high.

RIGHT

Clear plastic "popsicle." Extended dome and white oval-footed base. Back of dome painted blue, silver glitter. Base reads "China/No 764." Late 1980s. 4³⁄₁₆ in (10.5 cm) high.

ABOVE

Plastic drum. Base marked "No. 874/Made in Hong Kong," original sales label from "Gray Drugfair/$1.49," circa 1980s. 2¼ in (5.7 cm) diameter, 3¼ in (8.25 cm) high.

Extended dome shape. Clear plastic dome and white oval base, back of dome painted light blue, white snow. Base marked "logo P C in diamonds/AA 368/Made in Hong Kong." 1960s. 3½ in (8.9 cm) high.

Promotional snow globe. Clear plastic dome and white oval base, white snow. Back of snow globe painted dark blue. Base marked "Made in China." 1991. 2⅜ in (6 cm) high.

Clear plastic egg-shape. White plastic "eggshell" top and bottom, toned snow. Base marked "Enesco/Designed Giftware/© 1989 Enesco Corporation/Made in China." 2⅞ in (7.5 cm).

with a round base and a plastic dome that tapers almost to a point. These snow globes are known as "bullet" globes because the globe shape resembles the blunt end of a bullet. Another form has a rounded base, much like an egg, but with a distinct conical top.

Cylinder The principal cylindrical form is the drum snow globe. Often the cylinder approach is used in figural and shaped snow globes.

Dome Next to the ball shape, the elongated-side, dome shape is the most commonly found snow globe. The dome snow globe can have either an oval or round base. Oval-based dome snow globes tend to be compressed in depth. A few have flat backs. An oval-based snow globe with a dome of extended height is known as a "popsicle."

Egg With the growing popularity of holiday theme snow globes, the egg shape has found favor for Easter snow globes. Non-Easter theme egg-shaped snow globes exist, but are not common.

Figural This category contains two groups of snow globes. The first are three-dimensional personalities, figures, and other objects

RIGHT
Snowman with a snow globe stomach. The snow globe features two units (an angel with a reindeer, and a row of pine trees). Clear plastic dome with white snow. Back of feet marked "CHINA." 1980s. 5½ in (14 cm) high.

ABOVE
Figural type snow globe. Clear plastic dome and white oval base, silver glitter. Three-dimensional lion sits on top of the globe. Base marked "No. 354 S/Made in Hong Kong." No date. 5¹⁄₁₆ in (13 cm) high.

ABOVE
Oval-shaped New York souvenir. Clear plastic oval viewing plate surrounded by white ring, blue plastic side, back, and feet, white snow. Back marked "No V633/ Made in Hong Kong." 1980s. 3¾ in (9.5 cm) wide, 3 in (7.6 cm) high.

LEFT
Figural Santa Claus snow globe with two-piece (front clear, back red) plastic snow globe as part of his head. The snow globe contains two molded panels and white snow. Back of Santa's jacket marked "logo 8843/Made in Hong Kong/U.K. Design Registration/No 1030309." Late 1980s. 4⅞ in (12.4 cm) high.

LEFT
Lantern-shaped snow globe with a molded figure of a child skating. Plastic, white snow, marked on bottom "No. 662/Made in Hong Kong." 2 × 2 × 4 in (5 × 5 × 10 cm).

ABOVE
Nativity scene with six molded figures on a platform. White footed base with a back panel of light blue plastic. Base marked "Made in Hong Kong/© No. 357." 1960s/70s. 3⅛ in (8 cm) wide, 2¾ in (7 cm) high.

LEFT
Kerosene lamp holds a molded Christmas tree in a glass-ball snow globe. Paper label reads "Enesco/Design Giftware/© 1989 Enesco Import Corp./Made in Taiwan R.O.C." 4⅝ in (11.75 cm) high.

in which the stomach or central area is a snow globe. A seated Mickey Mouse has a snow globe stomach featuring Snow White's castle. The second includes snow globes that have a plastic figure attached to their top or base.

SHAPED This is a catchall category for snow globes shaped like another object, such as a bell, candle, church, shoe, or treasure chest. Keep your eyes open for these. They make a great specialized collection.

RECTANGLE This category includes cube, rectangle, and similar shaped geometric snow globes. While a few independent cube snow globes can be found, many rectangular snow globes are incorporated as the principal decorative element in a shaped figure, like the screen of a television set.

NOTE

The key to determining the shape of a snow globe is to look at the viewing surface. With the exception of the bottle, figural, and shaped snow globes, the overriding consideration is the geometric shape.

ABOVE LEFT
Winter scene of a deer and three pine trees. Glass dome, black plastic base, and white snow. Base marked "Made in Austria." Erwin Perzy. 1980s. 4⅝ in (11.7 cm) high.

ABOVE RIGHT
An Italian souvenir featuring a standing image of Puccini. Pink-toned plastic ball, green plastic fluted bowl base, and white snow. Water stopper marked "27." Possibly made in Italy, late 1980s. 3⅞ in (9.75 cm) high.

RIGHT
Octagonal-paneled glass dome, with a wood base and white snow. Paper label on base reads Made in Taiwan." 1990s. 4⅜ in (10.6 cm) high.

RIGHT

A winter scene featuring four molded units. Clear plastic dome and white oval footed base, white snow. Snowflake plug on top. Base marked "Made in/Western Germany." Attributed to Siper. 1950s. 2¼ in (5.7 cm) high.

·········· CONTAINER ··········

The two principal substances used to make snow globe containers are glass and plastic. Most collectors do not discriminate. However, a small group of individuals favors glass globes over plastic ones, perhaps because the earliest snow globes were made of glass. Some collectors say glass snow globes simply "feel" different from plastic.

All containers must allow the easy insertion of the central figure or scenic panel, snow, and liquid and must have a seal that keeps evaporation to a minimum. Early snow globes used a variety of sealing methods. The ball snow globe is actually shaped much like a light bulb with the neck hidden by the base. A variety of substances ranging from tin to rubber served as seals, and effectiveness varied.

With the arrival of the plastic container, a variety of sealing methods were employed. Some 1950s German examples had a plug on top. Eventually, the plug moved to its present home in the bottom of the plastic base.

Many of these plugs are ineffective, and even when a plug is secure, some evaporation occurs. As snow globe collectors become more sophisticated, they are growing more tolerant of this natural phenomenon, especially in pre-World War II snow globes. Others are experimenting with reopening these globes and replacing the liquid – a procedure not advocated by all.

ABOVE

Hand-painted bisque figure of a U.S. Marine. Glass ball, black glazed ceramic base, white snow. Decal on base reads "Souvenir of/U.S. Marine Corps/Pariss Island, S.C." Atlas Crystal Works, Trenton base. 1941–43. 4⅛ in (10.5 cm) high.

LEFT
A party snow globe. Plastic dome and round base, two-color (silver obverse, red reverse) plastic snow. Distributed by Enesco. Made in Hong Kong, circa 1980s. 3⅜ in (8.5 cm) high.

ABOVE
Statue of Liberty souvenir backed by a clear plastic panel with a painted skyline. Glass ball, plastic sloping sided rectangular base, oil filled, silver glitter. Plastic weighted base. Attributed to Progressive. 1950s. 4 in (10 cm) high.

LIQUID

In addition to acting as a medium in which the snow can fall, the liquid in a snow globe sometimes also serves to magnify the central figure or panel scene. This works well in the ball shape, but relatively little effect is achieved in the dome shape.

Water is the liquid most commonly found in snow globes. Most manufacturers used a convenient, nearby water supply. Initially little concern was given to the purity of the water. Pollution was not a major problem in many areas during the last half of the 19th century and first part of the 20th century.

The situation changed dramatically in the 1960s when a series of snow globes imported from Hong Kong were found to contain polluted water. The manufacturer had taken water directly from Hong Kong harbor. Today the liquid used in snow globes is chemically treated to kill impurities.

In addition to these chemicals, glycol is added to the water to slow down the movement of the snow. Perzy, an Austrian manufacturer, adds antifreeze to prevent breakage when snow globes are shipped in cold weather. Other manufacturers ship their snow globes empty, relying on the warehouse or retailers to fill them prior to final sale.

Progressive Products, an American firm, used oil as a liquid in their snow globes, with marginal results.

Manufacturers carefully guard the exact nature and chemical balance of their liquids. It is considered a trade secret, something that would aid their competitors if they knew the exact mix.

One snow globe manufacturing problem is that of eliminating all air during the filling process. One manufacturer filled his balls under water in an effort to solve the problem. The liquid in snow globes also expands and contracts, due to temperature changes, etc. Atlas Crystal Works placed a diaphragm in the bottom of their snow globes to compensate for this action.

ABOVE

Hand-painted bisque central figure of a boy holding a teddy bear. Glass ball, Bakelite base; snow has combined with chemicals in the water to produce brown fuzzy substance coating arms of boy and back of bear. Possibly American, late 1930s. 4¼ in (10.75 cm) high.

ABOVE RIGHT

A Halloween monster figure. Clear plastic dome and black oval base, snow in the shape of bones. Base marked "Enesco/©." Paper label reads "Enesco/Design Gift Ware/© Made in Hong Kong." 1980s. 3¼ in (8.25 cm) high.

········· SNOW (FLITTER) ·········

Just as manufacturers seek the ideal liquid mix with which to fill a snow globe, they also search for the ideal snow. No universally successful solution exists. Commercial manufacturers continually try new formula and substances. Collectors have experimented with everything from ground-up moth balls to crushed sand dollars. The search continues.

A wide variety of materials were used in early snow globes. Manufacturers tried bone chips, ceramic and pottery fragments, minerals, ground rice, sand, sawdust, and wax bound with camphor. Was the use of ceramic and pottery fragments one of the first instances of recycling?

Because of the wide variety of materials used to make snow, problems have arisen in a number of older snow globes. In many instances the snow has turned tan or brown in color. In some globes, the snow has clumped together. In other globes a fuzzy growth has developed on the snow and has often settled onto the central bisque figure.

Most collectors like to play with their snow globes, and are more concerned with owning working domes than preserving period accuracy. As a result, the initial temptation is to restore the globe by removing the deteriorated snow and replacing it. Think carefully before making this choice. Snow globe collecting is in its

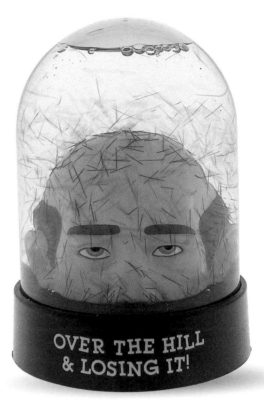

ABOVE
New England Collectors' Society limited edition. Hand-painted injection-molded figure of Scrooge McDuck. Glass dome, wood base, silver circles as snow. Paper label on base reads "NE/ The First/Limited Edition/ Disney/Crystal/Snow Globe Collection/Scrooge/McDuck/© Disney." 1990. 4³/₁₆ in (10.5 cm) high.

ABOVE RIGHT
The top half of a man's head peers through a colorless plastic dome and over a round black base. "Snow" formed by strands of black hair. Base marked "Enesco/Designed Giftware/ © 1987 Enesco Corporation/Made in China." 1987. 4³/₄ in (12 cm).

infancy. As snow globe collecting matures, premium prices will be paid for unaltered domes. Do not do something now that you may regret later.

In the post-World War II period, snow globes began to rain a host of other materials in addition to white snow. The most common is a plastic glitter. The square pieces are cut very small and often have a color (red and green are the most popular) on one side and a silver sheen on the other. Recently, plastic glitter has also been given an iridescent quality.

Plastic snow in a variety of shapes and colors can be found in snow globes dating from the early 1980s. Snow comes in balls, bats (the flying kind), hearts, stars, and a plethora of realistic shapes. A businessman sitting on the bottom of a snow globe is in seventh heaven as a stream of green dollar bills floats down the above. A Halloween dome contains a trick-or-treat bag into which imitation candy corn pieces drop.

The key element in the technology of any snow globe is prolonging the length of time it takes for the snow to fall. One method of controlling this process is the density of the liquid, another the shape of the snow. Some shapes fall faster than others. Shake a few globes and observe the rate of fall. You will be surprised at the differences that you encounter.

ABOVE

Hand-painted bisque figure of a girl standing beside a duck and holding a carrot. Glass ball, Bakelite base, white snow. Unknown maker. 1930s. 4¼ in (10.75 cm) high.

ABOVE RIGHT

Hand-tinted black and white photograph forms the panel. Glass dome, Bakelite base, white snow. Decal label on base. Maker unknown. Late 1930s. 4⅛ in (10.4 cm) high. (Restored).

·········· FIGURE OR PANEL SCENES ··············

The only limit to the material used for the central figure or panel scene in a snow globe is that it does not dissolve in the liquid. Snow globe figurines have been found in bisque (unfired porcelain), bone, a wide variety of metals, minerals, molded plastic, rubber, and wax.

In snow globes made before 1940, a central figure, often standing alone, was dominant. This figure could be a real or fictional individual, object, building, or scene. Figures often were painted to provide color. Independent backgrounds were rare.

Positioning the figures and scenic panels properly presented problems. In some cases small wooden wedges were used. William M. Snyder of Atlas Crystal Works patented a system using flanges and notches on the figure and mounting base.

In the 1930s and 1940s American snow globes appeared with a photographic background. American purchasers loved the realistic nature of these images. Italian manufacturers countered with printed or painted cutout silhouettes of villages, landscapes, and other scenes.

The quality of the central figure or panel scene, the placement, and the manufacture of the container and base of pre-1940 snow globes serves as the standard by which all later globes are judged.

LEFT
A New York souvenir with five panels (Empire State Building, Statue of Liberty, World Trade Center, New York skyline, clouds). Clear plastic dome and white oval-footed base, back of dome painted dark blue, silver glitter. Base marked "Made in Hong Kong/No. 354." 1970s. 3⅛ in (8 cm) high.

ABOVE
Lucite panel with a decal of Mt. Rushmore. Clear plastic dome and white oval base, back of dome painted light blue, white snow. Base marked "Made in Hong Kong/No. 352V." 1990s. 2¼ in (5.7 cm) high.

They represent the golden age of snow globe manufacture, but not of snow globe production. The heyday of snow globe production was the 1950s and 1960s.

As in many other industries, the technological advances of World War II brought significant changes. The development of plastic and injection-molding techniques created scope for a host of new shapes and interiors. Unfortunately, it also widened the quality level of the finished product. Collectors of post-war snow globes are beginning to develop criteria for separating desirable from less desirable plastic examples.

After World War II scenic backgrounds became commonplace. Plastic injection molding opened the door to a variety of new approaches from diecut backgrounds to multilayered scenes. Hand painting remained the principal means of applying color. By the 1950s plastic figures were used in most snow globe production.

The arrival of an elaborate ornamental scenic background paved the way for the dominance of the dome shape. No longer was a snow globe meant to be viewed from a three hundred and sixty-degree angle. A dome-shaped snow globe with a fixed scene can correctly be viewed only from the front. Following the lead of Koziol, a German firm, several manufacturers began painting a blue field behind the central figure or panel scene. For the traditionalist collector, much of the fascination of the snow globe was lost due to this innovation.

The 1960s witnessed the introduction of snow globes with mechanical action. A mechanical-action snow globe was not a new

RIGHT

A holiday souvenir from Hawaii. Clear plastic dome with white oval base, back of dome painted blue, silver glitter. Base marked "No 844/Made in Hong Kong/B." 1980s. 3 in (7.6 cm) high.

ABOVE

A model of Star Trek's U.S.S. Enterprise suspended on a lucite rod. Glass ball, plastic base and rotating hood, green glitter. Made in China, 1992. 7 in (17.75 cm) high, box – 7½ in × 7½ in × 9 in (19 × 19 × 22.8 cm). Base marked: "Hallmark Authorized User/Willitts Designs, Item No. 47051, NCC 1701 Lighted Star Globe." One of a series of three limited-production Star Trek editions, each limited to twelve months of production.

idea. Modern Novelty of Pittsburgh, Pennsylvania, produced several action water-filled globes in the late 1920s, but the concept failed to attract a large audience and was short-lived. The 1960s mechanical action revival gained immediate favor and continues to influence design in the 1990s.

The earliest 1960s mechanicals featured airplanes, balloons, seaweed, and railroad trains. Many were bobbing objects attached to a fixed string. Seesaw and other lever-action objects quickly followed. Modern inexpensive snow globes continue this tradition. No major new advances have occurred. Contemporary manufacturers of limited editions use other features, such as the introduction of a music box, to enhance the value of a snow globe.

Hand-painted bisque figure of an elephant on a platform. Glass dome, black glazed ceramic base, white snow. Atlas Crystal Works, Trenton, base. 1941–43. 4⅛ in (10.5 cm) high. (Restored).

ABOVE
Hand-painted bisque figure of a bear on a sloping hillock. Glass dome, Bakelite base, white snow. Base marked "Made in U.S.A./ U.S. Patent/logo (SB Co.)/ 7/5282." Maker unknown. 1939–40. 4³⁄₁₆ in (10.5 cm) high. (Restored).

One additonal feature must be mentioned – the introduction of battery-powered lights to enhance or illuminate the central scene. The results have been greeted with mixed emotions by collectors. Some view it as the final cheapening of an already cheap product. Others see it as one more fascinating kitsch feature of snow globes.

BASE

Most snow globes rest on some kind of base. The exception is when the snow globe is incorporated into a figural design, such as the stomach of a human figure or the supporting base for a statue.

The earliest bases were made of glazed pottery clay. The favored glazes were black, very dark brown, and cobalt blue. Once again, collectors will encounter an endless variety of base materials: marble, metal, plastic, porcelain, pottery, and wood.

Base design differed regionally, especially on late 19th- and early 20th-century snow globes. Early French snow globes used a flat square base, one with little or no neck. Favored material was ceramic or marble. Check the marble carefully, it may be faux. Austrian and German snow globes were taller, and their bases utilized a slight pedestal.

Most bases for ball snow globes are of the pedestal variety. Shape varies. While some modern plastic dome-shaped snow globes have three or four ball feet attached to the base, the vast majority of bases rest flat. When a snow globe contains a music box within a wood or plastic base, feet are common.

The introduction of plastic as the primary material in the production of snow globes resulted in a major change in size.

ABOVE
Mountain Retreat. Hand-painted bisque figure in a glass ball. The base is hexagaonal paneled green glass. White snow. Base marked "D.R.G.M./Germany." No date. 3⅝ in (9 cm) high.

CLOSE, BUT NO CIGAR

In addition to snow globes, a number of water-filled ring-toss games appeared in the post-World War II period. Modern examples can be found in any large toy store. While snow globe collectors may include an example or two in their collection, these are definitely not snow globes. However, collectors will encounter banks, calendars, drinking glasses, key chains, and salt and pepper shaker sets that incorporate a snowstorm unit as part of their composition. Technically, they are all snow globes.

The purpose of a true snow globe is to entertain. There is nothing functional about it. It provides amusement, a brief respite from the hectic pressures of life. It brings joy. Linking this independence with a functional object changes the concept.

Yet, these functional snow globes cannot be ignored. Collectors include them in their collections, often displaying them apart from the rest of their snow globes.

Collectors in other categories faced with this problem utilize a "More Than Just A _____" approach. It is time to introduce this to snow globe collecting. Classify these oddities (we hesitate to call them novelties), as "More Than Just A Snow Globe."

ABOVE
Combination snow globe and ring-toss game. Hand-painted injection-molded green dinosaur with another dinosaur in background. Plastic dome with blue painted background, white snow, three rings. The object of the game is to put rings around the dinosaur's neck. An applied sticker on the base reads "Abbeville Press." Made in Hong Kong, No. 352V. *Circa* 1991. 2 in (5 cm) high.

Older pedestal domes range in height from 3 to 4 inches (7.5 to 10 cm). The average height of a post-1950 plastic globe is 2½ inches (6.3 cm). Contemporary snow globes made for the mail-order market often exceed 6 inches (14.5 cm) in height.

Collectors of contemporary souvenir snow globes find the location information incorporated in the central scene. In older snow globes, especially pre-World War II examples, this information was frequently found on the base. In many cases, mishandling and cleaning has removed the attached souvenir label. When this happens, the value of the snow globe is reduced. A fun collection, albeit one that will require a great deal of persistence, is to find examples of the same snow globe with a different souvenir label attached to each base. It can be done.

ABOVE
Mechanical souvenir snow globe. Clear plastic dome and white oval-footed base, back of dome painted light blue, white snow. Base marked "No. 752/Made in Hong Kong." 1960s/70s. 2⁵⁄₁₆ in (6 cm) high.

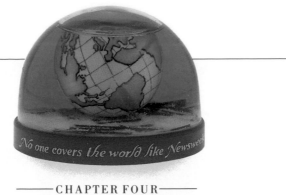

No one covers *the world like Newsweek*

CHAPTER FOUR

A SNOW
GLOBE ODYSSEY

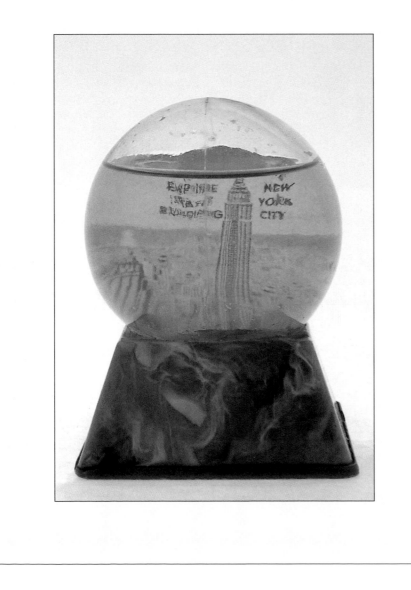

TOP
Clear plastic dome with red oval base, white snow and red panels. Back of snow globe painted blue. Base marked "logo NO 8813/ Made in Hong Kong." Late 1980s. 3⅛ in (8 cm) high.

LEFT
Tinted photograph of the New York skyline. Glass ball, plastic sloping rectangular base, white snow, oil filled. Base marked "Made in U.S.A," attributed to Progressive. 1950s. 4¹/₁₆ in (10.2 cm) high.

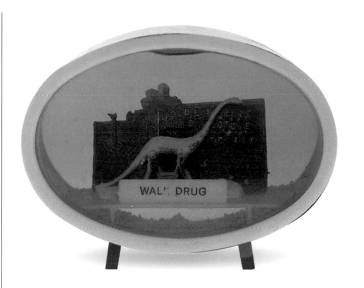

Two hand-painted, injection-molded units. Identification plate reads "Wall Drugs." Clear plastic oval viewing surface surrounded by white plastic ring. Blue plastic body, back, and legs, white snow. Marked on back "No. V633/Made in Hong Kong." Late 1980s. 3⅝ in (9 cm) wide, 2¾ in (7 cm) high.

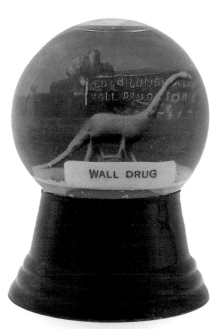

Another promotional item from Ted and Bill Hustead. Plastic ball and base, back half of ball light blue plastic. Base marked "Made in Hong Kong." No date. 4¼ in (10.75 cm) high. This globe was not given away as a premium. You had to buy it.

A collector's snow globe odyssey begins the minute he or she makes that fateful decision to acquire a first snow globe as an adult. A snow globe souvenir catches the eye. Perhaps the collector spots a childhood snow globe treasure at a flea market or antiques show and cannot resist recapturing the past. A snow globe from long ago that survived by hiding in the back of a drawer or an old shoe box is rediscovered. Whatever the reason, the journey commences.

One snow globe quickly gives way to many. What began as a small display on a shelf or in a cupboard can threaten to overrun the entire house or office.

Snow globe collectors quickly learn that they will never own one of every snow globe ever produced. There are thousands of shapes and motifs. Add variations, and the number doubles.

Every collector faces a number of limiting factors — affordability, availability, personal financial constraints, and space. These restraints do not deter collectors — they merely force them to face the reality that they must limit their collecting to a few select topics. They still participate in a snow globe odyssey; it just covers a slightly smaller territory than they might prefer.

Most collectors, in the early stages of their collecting, tend to be very eclectic — a little of this, a little of that; buy everything in sight. As the collector meets, talks, and visits with other collectors, interests are refined.

The early eclectic stage serves snow globes collectors well. As collectors identify the collecting categories in which they will specialize, their non-related snow globes became important

trading stock. A typical snow globe collector increases his or her collection as much by trading as by purchase.

Just as there is virtually no limit to the number of snow globe motifs, there is also no restraint on how collectors define the snow globe journey they will undertake. The most commonly selected routing focuses on a specialized topic. However, before departing for a list of topical ports, three other collecting focuses deserve mention: chronological time periods, country of origin, and manufacturer or distributor. The first can be done only in broad terms since an exact manufacturing date is known for only a few snow globes. Country of origin is often indicated on snow globes manufactured for export, but not on those for sale within the country of origin. Many manufacturers and distributors failed to include their names on their snow globes, so attribution is often more guesswork than fact. The end result is that chronological time periods, country of origin, and manufacturer or distributor have met with relatively little favor as collecting topics.

The most logical itinerary for our odyssey begins with "A" and winds its way through the alphabet. Stop as long as you like along the way, and remember that the trip covers only a few highlights. It is up to you to identify, plan, and travel the byways.

·················· ADVERTISING ··················

There is a thin line between an advertising snow globe and a souvenir snow globe. Souvenir snow globes promote their location through the inclusion of an identification name plate and recognizable figure, structure, or site within the globe. In fact, they advertise their location. However, the key is that souvenir

LEFT
A rare Coca-Cola snow globe. Clear plastic dome and white oval footed base, white snow. Back of snow globe painted dark blue. Base marked "No. 352V/ Made in Hong Kong." 1960s. 2⁵⁄₁₆ in (6 cm) high.

ABOVE
A Florida souvenir. Clear plastic dome and oval ivory base. Silver glitter snow. Base marked "Ⓛ 601/Made in Hong Kong." 1960s. 4 in (10 cm) wide, 3⅛ in (8 cm) high.

ABOVE
Souvenir snow globe from Alaska. Clear plastic dome and white oval-footed base, back of dome painted blue, white snow. Base of dome reads "No. 352V/ Made in Hong Kong." 1970s. 2⅜ in (6 cm).

Oval ashtray with a snow globe. The globe contains a hand-tinted black and white photograph. Glass ball, white snow, decal on base. Bakelite ashtray marked "5222/3/logo (SB Co.)." 1939–40. Oval base – 5¹¹⁄₁₆ in × 4⁵⁄₁₆ in (14.5 × 11 cm).

ABOVE

The Guggenheim Museum at night and a hand-painted lucite panel with night stars. Clear plastic dome and black oval-footed base, back of dome painted dark blue, white snow. Made in Germany. 1992. 2½ in (6.3 cm). Bar coded price label for $12.00.

snow globes are purchased, often at a premium price; the "artist" snow globe series from the Guggenheim Museum in New York City which sell at double the cost of similar globes is one example.

An advertising snow globe is one that is received as a free gift. The key word is free. A company wishing to promote its product or services contracts for a specially produced snow globe which it then distributes to its clients.

Some advertising snow globes are distributed as point of purchase or proof of purchase products. You have to buy another product or number of products to qualify to receive the snow globe; but, in theory, you receive the snow globe free.

A gray area exists in respect to snow globes that are received as rewards. It may be true that the recipient did not have to pay for the snow globe and that it contains a company's logo and/or other form of company information, but if the snow globe was not intended specifically for advertising purposes, it is not an advertising snow globe.

·············· AMERICA THE BEAUTIFUL ··············

One of the favorite approaches is to obtain one snow globe from each of the fifty states. Sounds easy, but it is not. The smaller states such as North and South Dakota, Rhode Island, and Delaware offer limited possibilities. Collections numbering in the hundreds can be developed for individual states, especially for tourist states such as Florida.

Hand-painted bisque figure of a penguin. Glass dome, Bakelite base, white snow. Maker unknown. Early 1950s. 4³/₁₆ in (10.5 cm) high. (Restored).

A mechanical souvenir snow globe. Clear plastic dome and white oval-footed base, back of dome painted blue, silver glitter snow. Base marked "Made in Hong Kong: NO. 202." 1960s/ 70s. 2³/₈ in (6 cm) high.

Take almost any subtopic, apply an American twist, and, you have a collecting category. Collect snow globes from famous Revolutionary War sites, tourist attractions, state capitols, major metropolitan areas, mountain resorts – the list goes on and on.

THE ANIMAL KINGDOM

Where do you stop? When a category is broad enough to cover domesticated animals, birds of the air, fish of the sea, beasts of the jungle, and zoological inmates, do you have extra shelves or cupboards to handle the overflow? One collection I know includes only snow globes with three-dimensional plastic animal figures attached – it contains over one hundred examples.

Collecting animal-related snow globes requires close scrutiny. In some animal theme snow globes, the animal, primarily a cat, is the central figure, but most animals are simply part of the background scene. While you can find plenty of snow globes with a reindeer in the background, it is difficult to find a snow globe that features a reindeer as the central figure.

Equally challenging is finding representations that are specific, rather than general. Birds and fish in snow globes tend to be generic representations. Mammals look more like themselves.

BY THE SEA

When vacation time arrives, most people head either for the mountains or the ocean. While there are plenty of mountain theme snow globes, they pale in number to those touting popular seaside resorts and beaches, and the sea has always fascinated collectors.

Most seaside snow globe collectors focus on ocean resorts. However, one can assemble a specialized collection of snow globes by focusing on resort hotels, beach scenes, bathing beauties, or sailing. Most of the seaside snow globes date from after World War II. One group of collectible snow globes, many Italian in origin, have bases with ornamental seashell displays. Interesting largely for their kitsch value, they are funky and definitely an acquired taste.

CATS

Given the fact that cats are the most collectible animal generally, it is surprising that there are not more cat-theme snow globes. Cat collectors purr contentedly if they acquire four to six new globes a year featuring the beloved animal.

Meeeouch!

RIGHT
Injection-molded cat with its tail caught in a fan. Plastic dome and oval base, hair-shaped snow. Designed by John Jonik in 1989 for Enesco Corporation. Made in China. Oval base 4½ × 3¼ in (11.4 × 8.25 cm), 3⅞ in (7.5 cm) high.

ABOVE
New England Collectors' Society limited edition. Mickey Mouse as The Sorceror's Apprentice. Glass dome, wood base, silver stars as snow. Paper label on base reads: "NE/First/Limited Edition/ Disney/Crystal/Snow Globe Collection/Mickey Mouse/© Disney." 1990. 4³⁄₁₆ in (10.5 cm) high.

Within cat collecting, the vast majority of the snow globes are contemporary, made in the last twenty years. Any cat snow globe made before 1970s is considered scarce, and those predating 1945 are very rare indeed.

Most cat collectors care little about the origins of the cat being portrayed, but they do want a positive portrayal of their feline friends. Although the vast majority of cat snow globe collectors are generalists, there are a few specialized collectors for character cats such as Garfield, storybook cats like Puss in Boots, and the Halloween black cat.

················· CARTOON CHARACTERS ·················

This category is heavily nostalgia-driven. Collectors everywhere want to recapture favorite childhood memories, and parents and grandparents want to make certain their heirs experience their own image of an idyllic childhood moment.

Many of these snow globes, such as Monogram Products Disney series, date after 1970. Serious collectors focus on snow globes that are licensed for specific characters. There is a difference between a Disney-licensed Snow White snow globe and a generic Snow White panel based solely upon the fairy tale.

This is one collecting subcategory where the snow globe collector competes actively with outside collectors. Many examples are priced at levels that are prohibitive in the eyes of the snow globe community. Patience is critical in the hunt. Because these snow globes are mass-produced, you should eventually find one at a price you can afford.

Hand-painted plastic snowman with a snow globe in his stomach. The globe features two hand-painted, injection-molded panels. White snow. Back of snowman marked "Made in Hong Kong/ No. 8025." No date. 5½ in (14 cm) high.

Plastic standing Santa figure. In his stomach is a snow globe containing a hand-painted injection-molded elf figure with a lamp walking through a pine forest. White snow. Marked on back "Made in Hong Kong/No. 8824," circa 1980s. 5⅝ in (14.25 cm) high.

Mary with the Christ Child, and a glittered roof outline and tree. Clear plastic dome and white footed oval base, back of dome painted dark blue, outside of base painted gold, white snow. Base marked "Made in Hong Kong." 1960s. 2⅞ in (7.5 cm).

·················· CHRISTMAS ··················

This category is so large that a complete collection would number in the thousands, especially if it includes any snow globe with a winter motif. The only way to survive is to specialize immediately.

Some suggested areas of snow globe specialization are Christmas carolers, living room (Christmas tree and hearth) scenes, music box snow globes that play Christmas tunes, North Pole, Rudolph the Red-Nosed Reindeer, Santa Claus (Father Christmas), Santa's elves, sledding scenes, and snowmen. Alas, what is missing is a wealth of snow globes featuring the Nativity scene.

This is one of the fastest-growing snow globe collecting categories. Many of the contemporary globes are distributed by firms involved in the trim-a-tree industry. As a result, they introduce their largest number of snow globes for the Christmas season, and most have a Christmas theme.

·················· FAMOUS FACES ··················

You might think that it is easy to find snow globes whose central motif is an important historical, military, political, or religious figure. Not true. This is a category where you really have to hunt.

A working checklist compiled from snow globes illustrated in Nancy McMichael's *Snowdomes* includes: James Dean, Goldwater and Miller (1964 Republican American presidential candidates), Gorbachev, Charles Lindbergh, General MacArthur, Marilyn Monroe, and Pope John Paul II. A few reward snow globes contain

LEFT
A satirical snow globe; portrait of Margaret Thatcher. Clear plastic dome and round gray footed base, silver needle snow. Made in West Germany. 1980s. 3³/₁₆ in (8 cm) high.

ABOVE
Elvis at Graceland. Two-part plastic dome (front clear, back blue), red pedestal with white base plate, silver glitter. Base marked "Made in Hong Kong/ No. 335 A." 1980s. 3⁹/₁₆ in (9 cm) high. Paper price label for $3.99.

pictures of the recipients (or, at worst, the company founder). Of course, you can add your name to this list if you make your own snow globe that features your picture on it.

Fairy-tale and legendary figures such as Smokey the Bear or Paul Bunyan, snow globes featuring the "homes" of personalities, or generic types such as an English Beefeater cannot be included in your personality collection. Only "real" people truly belong in this category.

···················· FOREIGN TRAVEL ····················

What is foreign is relative. This category includes snow globes from nations other than the one in which you live. Again, the only limiting factor is your imagination. How about: one from each continent, one from every country in Europe, South America, or other geographic region, foreign capitals, or famous festivals.

RIGHT
Venice. Two hand-painted, injection-molded silhouette panels (a gondola and St. Mark's Cathedral). Colorless plastic dome and white oval base, white snow. Base marked "Made in China." 1990s. 4¹/₈ in (10.5 cm) wide, 3 in (7.6 cm) high.

A fairytale picture: a princess and a frog. Clear plastic dome and white oval-footed base, back of dome painted light blue, white snow. Base marked "3/1072/Ges. Gesch 1675631." No date. 2½ in (6.3 cm) high.

Bisque bust portrait of General Douglas MacArthur. Glass ball, black glazed ceramic base, white snow. Decal label on base. Atlas Crystal Works, Trenton base. 1941–43. 4⅛ in (10.5 cm) high.

Smart collectors focus on snow globes that picture identifiable buildings and scenes. This is another category where one generic scene panel covers a great deal of geographic territory.

You can of course enlist the help of friends and relatives. Just because you are not traveling abroad does not mean that you should forego a steady supply of snow globes from abroad. Ask your friends and relatives to pick up several of each example so you have extras for trading. After all, what are friends for?

FROGS

This category is included because one of the individuals who made snow globes available for photography is an ardent collector of frog snow globes. She is a princess who deserves to be kissed.

Her collection, which numbers close to one hundred, was assembled in less than ten years. Heavens knows how many snow globes she will have if she persists for another decade.

She proves the old adage in the antiques and collectibles field: one of everything exists. If you have never seen something, it is only because you have never looked. Collectors are among the most persistent people on earth. It is out there. And, they will find it, no matter what it takes.

GLOBES OF WAR

Snow globes went to war during 1939 to 1945 just like the world at large. Patriot snow globes featured individuals in military uniforms and inspiring patriotic motifs, such as flying flags and national symbols. Since most raw materials during this period went into the war effort, the number and variety of wartime snow globes is small.

Another approach is to focus on souvenir snow globes from famous battle sites. Collectors can concentrate on a specific war like the American Civil War, or try to secure an example relating to each war in which a country participated.

Overall, snow globe collecting is not sexist. There are an equal number of male and female collectors. The domes of war is the exception. It is definitely a male-dominated category.

HOLIDAY

As you have already discovered, Christmas is a category unto itself. "Holiday" snow globes include all the other holidays: Easter, Halloween, New Year, etc. If you focus on this category, you will have plenty of cause to celebrate.

ABOVE
A Halloween snow globe depicting a witch riding a broom. Plastic dome and round base. Two-color red and silver glitter snow. Marked on base "Russ/Russ Berrie & Co." Made in Hong Kong, 1980s. 3½ in (8.9 cm) high.

ABOVE
The example on the left is identical except that the identification plate has been turned upside down. Base marked "Made in Hong Kong." 1990s. 6⅜ in (15.75 cm) high.

RIGHT
In an egg-shaped snow globe, a hand-painted injection-molded bunny carries tulips. The container is glass with a painted wood base. Pink, blue, and white snow. Applied label on the bottom reads "Made in Taiwan/ R.O.C." 1990s. 3⅛ in (8 cm) high. One of a set of four made in Taiwan for Lillian Vernon, Mt. Vernon, NY 10550.

Consider this idea. Most collectors focus on the holidays celebrated in their country. American collectors eagerly seek 4th of July snow globes, a holiday of no meaning to a European. Dare to be different. Build a collection of snow globes that document holidays that are not celebrated in your own country.

Another collecting approach is to focus on important religious holidays. Europe is a fertile hunting ground for snow globes with this theme since many European globes have religious themes. A secondary approach is to develop a collection that shows religious holidays from different faiths.

···················· MISTAKES ····················

Talk about a fun category. It is hard to keep from laughing when you encounter these amusing snow globes. City landscapes turned upside down, words misspelled, wrong attributions, and objects that float in ways their designer never expected. The number of miscues is in the hundreds.

The majority of these mistakes result from foreign production. Words are easily mistranslated and misspelled. Workers at the plant who assemble the snow globes are unfamiliar with the scene or figure upon which they are working. Pirating also contributes to the problem. Perhaps mistakes are made deliberately to avoid copyright.

Never pass up a mistake snow globe. If you do not want it, there are plenty of other collectors who will gladly trade for it. Mistake snow globes are great conversation pieces and provide a moment of relief when viewing a large specialized collection.

The Eiffel Tower in Paris. Clear plastic dome and white oval-footed base, back of dome painted light blue, bottom of base marked ". . . Inhalt nicht zum Verzehr geeignet," paper label reads "Selection Bernard Carant/Paris/Made in Germany." 1991. 2⅞ in (7.5 cm) high.

Two-part plastic ball (front colorless, back light blue). The rectangular base has sloping sides with four "calendar" windows in the front, and a slot for money in the back. White plastic base marked "Made in Hong Kong/ VNO355L." No date. 4 in (10 cm) high.

·················· MONUMENTS ··················

Every country has several major architectural and historical monuments. Many are so well-known that no matter where a person lives, they easily identify them. Who would not recognize Paris's Eiffel Tower, Pisa's Leaning Tower, the Washington Monument or New York's Statue of Liberty.

While most collectors do not think of a snow globe as a form of historical document, it is. Some snow globes feature monuments, events, or cityscapes that no longer survive, such as an example with the central figure of the Trylon and Perisphere from the 1939–40 New York World's Fair. A small, but important snow globe collection would be one that focuses on lost history.

Since many of the featured monuments were constructed well in advance of the development of snow globes, it is common to find snow globes for the same monument from different decades. A collection could trace the development of snow globe design simply by assemblying a collection of snow globes that feature New York's Statue of Liberty. The current Eiffel Tower giftshop still sells Eiffel Tower snow globes, much as its 1889 counterpart did.

········ MORE THAN JUST A SNOW GLOBE ········

This is the category for the utilitarian snow globe, i.e., a snow globe that performs a specific function. The best known form is the snow globe salt and pepper shaker set. However, as more and more people become snow globe collectors, they are discovering a larger and larger variety of more-than-just-a-snow-globe objects.

A partial list includes ashtrays, bookcovers, calendars, Christmas tree ornaments, desk pen and pencil stands, drinking glasses, key rings, pens and pencils sets, pocket purses, and sugar shakers. No doubt you can add several more items to the list.

Do not confuse an item in this category with a snow globe lookalike, i.e. a glass object filled with liquid that contains no "snow." "The Original Melted Snowman" or the Florida snowman is housed in a water-filled, domed container, but the unit is not, by definition, a snow globe.

Also not included in this category is snow globe ephemera, shaped snow globes, and advertising and souvenir snow globes. The latter are designed and sold to promote a place and hence technically are functional objects. However, collectors do not view them in this fashion. Advertising, shaped, and souvenir snow globes are part of the mainstream of snow globe collecting.

·················· RELIGIOUS THEMES ··················

Religious snow globes divide into four main classes: biblical themes, religious shrines and holy sites, houses of worship, and religious personalities for example saints and popes. The vast majority have a European and Christian focus.

Biblical theme panels that illustrate Old and New Testament biblical passages exist, albeit the vast majority focusing on the life and death of Jesus Christ. Although globes predating 1945 can be found, most are from the post-war period.

Some of the earliest European snow globes were manufactured as religious site souvenirs. The Austrian manufacturer, Erwin Perzy, and the French manufacturer, Paul Viandel, are both noted for their religious motif snow globes. There are snow globes galore commemorating grottos, shrines, and religious retreats.

Snow globes were and still are popular souvenirs in church gift shops throughout the world. Most of the snow globes recognized by collectors feature the famous cathedrals of Europe, such as Chartres or Cologne. However, when James "Jimmy" Carter was president of the United States, the Plains Baptist Church of Plains, Georgia, could not resist the temptation of developing a snow globe souvenir of its building to sell to the tourists who flocked to Carter's hometown.

After a while, many of the saint snow globes start to look alike. Only the decal was changed to fool the innocent in far too many cases. A favorite subject for several decades has been the Pietà. A collection of a dozen or more globes could be assembled quickly, especially if you are willing to hop on a plane and do your hunting in Italy. What better excuse?

··················· SPORTS THEMES ···················

Virtually every major sport, from baseball to sailing, has been immortalized in a snow globe. Some present a serious portrayal; others focus on the humorous side. The principal problem in trying to assemble a collection of sport-theme snow globes is that the collector must compete against the participant whose family, relatives, and friends want him to have a small reminder of his affliction and the serious collector of anything that relates to his favorite sport topic.

Almost every collector approaches the subject by sport. Golfers collect golf snow globes; football fans collect football snow globes. The most commonly found sports snow globes portray either the

ABOVE
A biblical themed snow globe (Jesus and a disciple on water). Clear plastic dome and white oval-footed base, back of dome painted blue, white snow. Base reads "Made in Hong Kong." 1960s. 2¼ in (5.7 cm). Price label on bottom for $0.89.

ABOVE
Baseball snow globe (a batter on a diamond, and an aerial view of a stadium). Two-piece plastic ball (front clear, back light blue). Plastic sloping-sided rectangular base with Yankees logo, white snow. Base marked "Made in Hong Kong/C NO. 355." 1970s. 4¹⁄₁₆ in (10.2 cm) high.

ABOVE
Molded plastic panel of a couple in a Volkswagen convertible. Clear plastic dome and white oval-footed base, back of dome painted light blue, white snow. Made in Western Germany. 1980s. 2⁷⁄₁₆ in (6 cm) high.

ABOVE
Two injection-molded trucks on an oval disk suspended on a clear rod. Clear plastic hand-painted background of a cityscape. Glass ball, plastic sloping-sided rectangular base. Originally oil-filled, now filled with water. Plaster weighted base. Attributed to Progressive. 1950s. 4¹⁄₁₆ in (10.2 cm) high.

playing grounds or team logo. In both cases, interest is much stronger in the team's hometown than elsewhere for localized snow globes. The best buys are often found hundreds of miles away.

For those collectors seeking a broader-based collection, try a seasonal approach, such as snow globes that show winter sports. Surprisingly, very few Olympic-related snow globes have been discovered by collectors. Those that do exist are of recent origin.

TRANSPORTATION

From horse-drawn vehicles to space rockets, collectors can find a myriad of snow globes for virtually any form of transportation. Snow globes feature airplanes, automobiles, bicycles, buses, horse-drawn vehicles, motorcycles, ocean liners, people-drawn vehicles, trucks, sailing ships, and yachts.

The key in assembling a collection is to focus on the centrality of the vehicle. A true transportation snow globe has its principal focus on the vehicle. Concentrate as well on vehicles that can be specifically identified. A car that is a recognizable Cadillac or Mercedes Benz is more desirable than a generic type.

Snow globes that feature transportation terminals, such as airports and train stations, form an interesting secondary collection. Supplement your collection with snow globes from transportation museums.

THE WILD WEST

The wild west theme is universally loved around the globe, reinforced by the syndication of television shows, numerous western movies, and cowboy novels.

The American west, the place of six-gun heros and tall tales, subdivides into a number of collecting categories: the west of the Native American, the west of the Spanish and Mexican settlers, the real west of the working cowboy, the dude-ranch west of the tourist, and the fictional west of books, movies, and television, also known as the TV-cowboy west. All have been captured for images in snow globes.

In addition, the modern west of large metropolitan cities such as Denver, Las Vegas, and Phoenix and great national parks like Grand Canyon and Yellowstone has not escaped the designers and distributors of snow globes. The area west of the Mississippi and east of the Rockies is vast. If you want to collect wild-and-woolly west snow globes, you have to think like the Texans – BIG.

LEFT

Souvenir of the New York World's Fair showing the Unisphere. Clear plastic dome and white oval footed base, back of dome painted light blue, white snow. Base marked "Unisphere Represented by [logo U.S.S.] United States Steel/© 1961 N.Y.W.F./Made in Hong Kong." 2½ in (6.3 cm) high.

ABOVE

Hand-painted bisque standing figure in native American costume. Glass ball, Bakelite base, white snow. Decal label on base reads "American Indian." Maker unknown. Late 1930s. 4³⁄₁₆ in (10.7 cm) high.

········· WORLD'S FAIR ·········

They do not seem to stage world's fairs like the 1964 New York World's Fair or Expo' 67 in Montreal, Canada, any more. Modern fairs do not generate the same degree of enthusiasm or support among the nations as their predecessors did. Although there was a desire, the United States could not marshal the finances or forces necessary to launch another world's fair on the hundredth anniversary of two of America's greatest world's fairs – the Centennial Exposition (1876) or Columbia Exposition (1893).

Fortunately for snow globe collectors, almost every world's fair, especially those after 1939, licensed one or more snow globes. Collectors can focus on obtaining a snow globe that commemorates a fair as a whole or seek out snow globes issued as souvenirs by individual fair pavilions. Because of strong competition with world's fair collectors, world's fair snow globes command a premium price, especially those for pre-1940 fairs.

Our snow globe odyssey has consisted of 20 rich ports of call, each offering a number of sites to visit. Numerous side trips were suggested, but not taken.

The wonderful thing about a snow globe odyssey is that everyone's trip is unique. No collector is content to travel the route taken by another. Collectors are first and foremost individuals.

Good luck with your snow globe journey. Bring home a lot of souvenirs for your collection and hopefully a duplicate or two to trade. Let us know when you return. We are looking forward to hearing all about your trip!

—CHAPTER FIVE—

CONTEMPORARY SNOW GLOBES

TOP

An Apollo astronaut. Clear plastic dome and white oval footed base, silver glitter. Base marked "No 354V/Made in Hong Kong." 1980s. 3 in (7.6 cm) high. Paper price label for $4.00.

LEFT

Souvenir from *The Phantom of the Opera* musical. Clear plastic dome and round black base. Silver and red glitter. Base marked "© 1986 The Really Useful Group, PLC/All Rights Reserved Worldwide/Licensee Enesco Corporation . . . Made in China." 3 1/8 in (8 cm) high.

ABOVE
Wooden music box with snow globe and a bisque figure. Snow globe holds a three-dimensional figure of Santa Claus with a map and sack, and a North Pole sign. The bisque figure is of a young girl on her knees writing a letter to Santa. Glass ball, white snow. Extended oval wooden base, paper label reads "Price/ Products/Taiwan/Bellmawr, N.J." 1990s. 8 in (20 cm) wide.

There is currently a snow globe renaissance. This started in the late 1980s when home shopping became trendy. Marketing gurus touted the advantages of direct, targeted selling. The number of mail-order catalogs mushroomed. These catalogs focus on fulfilling the wishes and desires of the middle and upper class. Catalog buyers search for the unique and unusual. Consumers are willing to pay handsomely for well-manufactured gifts that are a step above the ordinary. High quality, special feature snow globes fit nicely into this merchandising atmosphere.

Within the past five years, catalog retailers have enticed buyers with an endless supply of snow globes, some issued in limited editions. Prices begin around $25.00 and go higher, depending on the bell-and-whistle enhancements. Many of these new snow globes have music boxes in their base, extensive mechanical action, or other special features to increase their value in the eyes and minds of consumers.

The growing popularity of these moderately priced, contemporary, commercial snow globes attracted museum giftshop buyers and groups promoting special cause or event. The Smithsonian Institution now offers snow globes that relate to objects in their collection or feature stories that have appeared in *The Smithsonian* magazine. Although offered for sale on site, the vast majority of The Smithsonian's snow globes are sold through mail-order catalogs.

LEFT
The Galaxy Collection Waterball by Russ. A silver-colored injection-molded scene showing Apollo landing on the moon. Clear plastic dome and round silver base. Back of dome painted dark blue, silver glitter. Bottom of dome marked "Made in Hong Kong." Russ Berrie and Company, Oakland, New Jersey, Item No. 4093. 1990s. 4 in (10 cm) high, box – 3¾ in × 3⅝ in × 4¾ in (9.5 × 9.25 × 12 cm).

ABOVE
Smithsonian's A Winter Wonderland Snow Globe. Hand-painted, injection-molded figure of an old-fashioned girl carrying a Christmas tree. Glass dome, wooden base with music box that plays "Winter Wonderland," white snow. Made in Taiwan. 1990. 5¾ in (14.6 cm), box – 5⁵⁄₁₆ in × 5 in × 7 in (13.5 × 12.7 × 17.75 cm). One of a series of six.

Artists are also exploring the snow globe as a potential art form, and crafters are making their own snow globes. The John Michael Kohler Arts Center in Sheboygan, Wisconsin, mounted a special exhibit on snow globes, and other museums have included snow globes within larger exhibits. Articles about snow globes appear regularly in both general and trade periodicals. A price guide to collectible snow globes is reported close to publication.

What contemporary snow globes should you save? All collectors whose favorite collectible has contemporary counterparts faces this dilemma. Too frequently, the tendency is to avoid modern examples. They are not antiques, not even collectibles, as collectors define the term. Contemporary snow globes are desirables – collectible, but speculative. The problem is that in 50 to 75 years, they will be just as antique as the older snow globes in today's market.

Wise collectors buy contemporary snow globes selectively. Because of the wide choice, collectors focus first on examples with themes that fit their major collecting emphases. Next in importance are snow globes that are extremely well made and have special features or regional focus.

Because so many contemporary snow globes are purchased "new," the collecting condition standards that apply to snow globes made after 1980 are very different from those used to grade globes manufactured earlier. Post-1980 snow globes must be in excellent to near-mint condition to have any collector value.

Furthermore, the snow globe is considered incomplete unless it is accompanied by its original packaging. The original packaging can double the price of an older snow globe and adds ten to fifteen percent to the resale value of a modern one. The box often contains a colorful picture featuring the globe, its history, or information about the manufacturer not found on the snow globe itself.

With such a strong emphasis on condition and original packaging for contemporary snow globes, is it safe for the collector to display and play with them? Alas, the answer may well be "No" if they are viewed only as a long-term investment. If you do not care about the long term, handling them creates no problem. There is a simple solution, buy two – one to touch and one to store carefully away.

········ NEW COMMERCIAL SNOW GLOBES ··········

The February 1993 issue of *Selling Christmas Decorations* (Douglas Edgell Publications) served as the 1993 directory for the American trim-a-tree industry. The "Water Globes" listing includes the names of 53 distributors/importers/manufacturers of snow globes. Major firms such as Kurt S. Adler, Inc./Santa's World, Enesco Corporation, and Silvestri appear along side those of Flambo Imports, Norcrest, and B. Shackman & Co.

Like many companies, Silvestri issues a number of seasonal trade catalogs. A sampling of the company's 1993 snow globe offerings include: Spring 1993 catalog – 44 snow globes; Christmas 1993 catalog – 136 snow globes; Christmas Catalog

FanDome Snow Globes

Ron Kaiser is one of those rare individuals who found a way of combining his business with his hobby. While attending a Los Angeles Lakers basketball game, Ron went looking for a snow globe of his favorite team. None existed and an idea was born.

Kaiser approached professional sports managers with his idea of creating a series team snow globes. The reception was enthusiastic and FanDome was born.

The key to the success of FanDome was to make the snow globes interactive. In addition to creating a snowstorm, the user is challenged to score a field goal, home run, hockey goal, or basket, by twisting and shaking the dome. FanDomes have been produced for all the teams in America's National Football League, Major League Basketball, National Hockey League, and National Basketball Association. In addition, a series of domes have been issued for 21 American college teams. FanDomes are numbered by series and edition to add to their collectability.

FanDomes are carefully crafted, silk screen snow globes. Their well designed packaging is considered a "must save" by collectors. In addition, snow globe collectors also try to obtain an example of one or more of FanDomes display boxes.

FanDome, a division of the Kintra Group, has produced a number of limited edition advertising snow globes. Not sold publically, these are eagerly sought by collectors.

Ron Kaiser's personal collection of snow globes number over seven hundred. He and Ronnie, his wife, live in California.

LEFT

**FanDome. Penn State Nittany Lions, College Football.
Series No. I, Edition No. I. Made in China. 1991. 3 in (8 cm) high.
Note: College colors for Penn State should be blue and white.**

Supplement – 57 snow globes. The total is 237 individual snow globes. It would have been higher had a 1993 Halloween catalog been available. Without doing an exact count, it is safe to assume that there are over a 1,000 commercially produced snow globes available in the current market.

In the search for individuality in the modern snow globe world, manufacturers and distributors have introduced changes in snow globe size, greatly enhanced the internal presentation, added better and more sophisticated external features, and created a number of special issue snow globes, some of which relate directly to the collectibles market.

Size changes are occurring at both ends of the spectrum. Ball globes are increasing in size as the interior scenes become more elaborate. The miniature snow globe arrived in the 1980s and is now very much part of the market. The introduction of mechanical movement to the internal scene is a major advance. External figurines and other elements that complement the interior snow globe scene, are unified on a platform base. Perzy did a limited edition of 333 "Snow Over Vienna" snow globes that included a Swatch watch. The snow globe sold out in three weeks and sells in the current market at over ten times its retail price.

The growing appeal of snow globes has enticed a number of smaller firms into the market. FanDomes of Santa Monica, California, began by licensing rights from the National Football League to produce snow globes for each of the teams in the league. The company's product line expanded to include snow globes for professional basketball and hockey teams along with several college teams. Silverdale, Inc. (PO Box 1465, Coeur d'Alene, ID 83814) also offers custom-designed snow globes for several college teams, as well as Christmas and patriotic themes. Unique Productions (PO Box 715, Mokena, IL 60448) will put your personal picture in a musical snow globe. Nell Kirsch (4340 Willow Grove Road, Dallas TX 75220) crafts made-to-order globes featuring snow made from ground sand dollars. Ter-A-Don Novelties (3844 McIntyre, Eau Claire, WI 54703) is selling a "Desert Storm Snow Globe," with a musical version that plays the Star Spangled Banner.

A number of mail-order merchants, department stores, and museums are using a "limited edition" or "annual" snow globe as a marketing tool. In 1992 Neiman Marcus issued its fifth annual snow globe, a musical example with a Venetian theme.

ABOVE
Bumper sticker and postcards manufactured by Victor Bokas, 1992.

ABOVE
A nostalgic scene of a 1930s couple ice skating. Glass ball, wood base, white snow. Limited edition information on a paper label on the base, entitled "The Skaters' Waltz." 1992. 4¾ in (12 cm).

NEIMAN MARCUS SNOW GLOBES

Beginning with its 1988 Christmas catalog, Neiman Marcus, a major American department store with chain headquarters in Dallas, Texas, has offered a musical snow globe annually. This snow globe features a central figure which matches the catalog's cover art. The following is a list of snow globes and their designers currently in the series:

1988 – Celestial Visions *Andre Francois*
1989 – Peaceable Kingdom *David Everett*
1990 – Black Art. Ancestral Legacy
    Rip Wood
1991 – Untitled (Santa and his reindeer
    flying over every roof to deliver a shower
    of puppies and kittens)
    Andreina Parpajola
1992 – Untitled (Santa in gondola)
    John Bombola

In addition to the snow globe the cover theme is used in a number of other products ranging from lithographed tin candy containers to note paper. In 1992 Neiman Marcus issued a set of four snow globe 12-ounce double Old Fashion tumblers. "The acrylic tumblers are double-walled. Shake the glasses, and celestial elements tumble about in the walled-in fluid."

ABOVE

1992 Neiman Marcus snow globe. Glass globe, wooden footed base with music box that plays "O Sole Mio." Two-tone (green/gold) glitter and stars. Based on a design by John Rombola. Made in **Taiwan. Ball 4¾ in (12 cm) diameter, 6¼ in (16 cm) high. On either side are the Old Fashion tumblers also by John Rombola. 3⅜ in (8.5 cm) diameter, 4¾ in (12 cm) high, sold as a set of four.**

Accompanying the snow globe was a matched set of snow globe glasses.

As more and more collectors began buying contemporary snow globes, several stores and mail-order catalogs specializing in snow globes have evolved. Two of these firms are Global Shakeup (2265 Westwood Blvd., #618, Los Angeles, CA 90064) and Toy Krazy (PO Box 281, Galloway, OH 43119).

Several private individuals and museums are active in the snow globe ephemera market. In 1990 the Museum of Modern Art in New York, New York, sold a snow globe theme Christmas card designed by Steven Guarnaccia. Victor Bokas (300 E. Hampshire #3, Orlando, FL 32804) sells snow globe bumper stickers and postcards. Snow globe notes and a "Christmas in the City" paper

ABOVE
Glossy paper shopping tote bag, bottom marked "Duro Designers/paper and plastics," 8 × 9 in (20 × 30 cm) folded. Designed and marketed by Louisville Central Area, Kentucky – a group of business representatives that promote the city's downtown area.

shopping bag can be purchased from *Snow Biz* (PO Box 53262, Washington, D.C. 20009). The "Christmas in the City" shopping tote was designed and marketed initially by the Louisville Central Area, Louisville, Kentucky, a group of business representatives who promote downtown Louisville. Nikta (305 40th Street, Sacramento, CA 95819) creates personalized snow globe theme stationery and postcards. Snow globe T-shirts and sweatshirts are available from P Street Paperworks (2412 18th Street, NW, Washington, D.C. 20009).

·········· MAKE YOUR OWN SNOW GLOBE ··········

More and more individuals are making their own snow globes. Your local art supply store has or can easily order the materials that you need. If unsuccessful, write National Artcraft Company (23456 Mercantile Road, Beachwood, OH 44122) for a copy of their direct mail catalog. The company offers ball and egg-shaped globes, a variety of bases (some with music boxes), snow globe trim-a-tree ornaments, silicone adhesive, and a variety of "drifting bits" ranging from white snowflakes to multicolor pastel and iridescent white glitter flakes.

Individuals who do not want to sculpt their own central figures can contact Scioto Ceramic Products (2455 Harrisburg Pike, Grove City, OH 43123) and Doc Holliday Molds (125 McArthur Court, Nicholasville, KY 40356) for a list of molds.

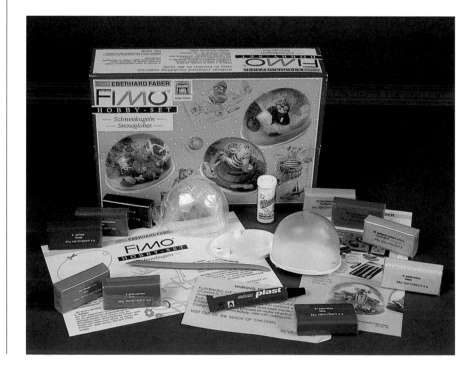

LEFT
Eberhard Faber FIMO Hobby-Set, 1992. Contains enough material to make two snow globes.

The 1992 F.A.O. Schwartz's "The Ultimate Toy Catalogue" offered a "FIMO" snow globe kit manufactured by Eberhard Faber GmBH of Neumarkt, Germany. FIMO is a molding clay brand name. The kit contains enough molding clay and parts to make two plastic, oval base, dome-shaped snow globes. The instruction sheet, in English and German, is easy to follow.

·············· SNOW GLOBES ON EXHIBIT ··············

From October 27, 1991, to February 2, 1992, the John Michael Kohler Arts Center in Sheboygan, Wisconsin, presented an exhibit entitled *Snowbound: The Enduring Magic of Snowdomes*. This pioneering exhibit featured 70 commercially made snow globes and 23 contemporary snow globes created by eight artists invited to take part in the exhibition.

The artists who participated in SNOWBOUND were among the first contemporary artists to explore the use of the snow globe as an artistic medium. While some artists incorporated themes from their previous work, others explored new ground.

Doug Baldwin of Baltimore, Maryland, created three duck-theme snow globes. The piece involved four snow globes, one for each year, with dollar-bill flitter. Each successive globe had fewer bills. The whole rotated on a musical box base that played "It's a Small World."

Artist William Bernstein of Brunsville, North Carolina, created his snow globes from handblown glass. The other artists who participated in the exhibit were Karen Breschi of San Francisco, California; Dave Quick of Los Angeles, California; Tom Rauschke and Kaaren Wiken from Palmyra, Wisconsin; Mark Soppeland of Akron, Ohio; and Rhonda Zwillinger of Brooklyn, New York.

The John Michael Kohler Arts Center has published a catalog for SNOWBOUND that illustrates the snow globes exhibited. Further information can be obtained by writing to JMKAC, PO Box 489, Sheboygan, WI 53082.

The Children's Museum of Manhattan (Tisch Building, 212 West 83rd Street, New York, New York) included snow globes as part of its "Great Stuff" exhibit held during the winter of 1992. Several collectors have worked with local public libraries to arrange a display of their collections.

Snow globe exhibiting is in its infancy. Collectors are already talking of the possibility of a snow globe museum. Expect to see a great deal more attention paid to snow globes in the years ahead.

ABOVE
Celebration by Karen Breschi. Pink curlers, reminiscent of the 1950s, fill the globe; the base is covered with found objects. 1991. 23 × 9½ × 9½ in (58 × 24 × 24 cm).

ABOVE
Where Lost Things Go by Mark Soppeland. Glass dome, walnut base, and glitter flitter. The black hole where all lost things seem to disappear. 1991. 7½ × 6 × 6 in (19 × 15 × 15 cm).

CHAPTER SIX

KEYS TO

COLLECTING

SNOW GLOBES

TOP

Germany. Two hand-painted, injection-molded units. The ship moves in a track. Clear plastic dome and white oval base, back of dome painted blue, white snow. Base marked "HONG KONG." 1980s. 2⅜ in (6 cm) high.

LEFT

Santa Claus holding onto a lamp post, the top of which features a square snow globe that features an angel and a reindeer. White snow. Base marked "© 1978 Brite Star Mfg. Co./Phila. PA. 19148/Made in Hong Kong." 5⅜ in (13 cm) high.

LEFT

A fish swimming through coral. Glass ball, plaster base in seashell and coral motif, green iridescent glitter. Made in Taiwan. 1990. 6⅛ in (15.5 cm) high; box – 5¾ in × 5¾ in × 7 in (14.6 × 14.6 × 17.75 cm). One of a series of six.

ABOVE

Hershey Kisses Tower and Sky Ride. Clear plastic "popsicle" extended dome with a white oval base. Back of dome painted blue, white snow. 1980s. 3⁷⁄₁₆ in (8.5 cm) high. A paper label on the bottom indicates a purchase price of $1.29.

Y ou have now read about the component parts of a snow globe, the history of snow globes, suggested topical approaches to collecting snow globes and the state of the contemporary snow globe market. Is there anything left before you hop in your car and begin the collecting process?

Unfortunately, the answer is yes. You need the keys to the collecting process. These keys open doors that will save you time and provide you with collecting skills that others learn only through the school of "hard knocks" and years spent collecting. It is certainly worth a few minutes to change yourself from a novice into a seasoned veteran.

COLLECTING KEY #1 –
⋯⋯ DEVELOP A COLLECTING PHILOSOPHY ⋯⋯⋯

Sit down and ask yourself what snow globes turn you on. The real fun in collecting is to collect what you like, not what someone else has suggested is the "right" or "smart" thing to collect. Because snow globes fall into the category of kitsch collectibles, whatever themes you collect, they are acceptable to other snow globe collectors and the outside world as well.

Several factors shape a collecting philosophy – storage space, finances, time, and availability. Not all snow globes are created equal – some are larger than others, especially many of the modern ones. Look carefully at how much space you have available and where it is located. How many globes will fit into it? Admittedly, the true collector totally discounts space. "There is always room

ABOVE
Hand-painted bisque figure of a leaping stag. Glass dome, Bakelite base, white snow. Decal label on base. Maker unknown. 1950s. 4⅛ in (10.4 cm) high. (Restored).

for one more" is the principle. Not everyone has this luxury.

Finances must play a major consideration. Common snow globes from the pre-1940 period are priced in the $35.00 to $60.00 range. Harder-to-find snow globes and snow globes whose motifs cross into other collecting categories can exceed $100.00. Snow globe collectors continually balk at these prices, but their outside rivals do not. All too often these domes find their way into the hands of dealers whose sole motivation in selling is maximum profit. If you cannot afford to pay the price, focus your attention elsewhere – it's not worth the heartache.

Contemporary special edition and seasonal snow globes begin at $25.00 and the prices go up and up. Several are priced above $100.00. These more expensive globes feature bells and whistles. Technological enhancements may turn off many snow globe collectors. Remember, a music box snow globe usually has more appeal to music-box or theme collectors than it does to snow globe collectors.

Plastic snow globes from the 1950s through the 1980s are still affordable. The vast majority of older examples sell in the $3.00 to $10.00 range. Many can still be found at garage sales and some flea markets for less than $1.00.

Once you get hooked on snow globes, it is addictive. Snow globe collecting is not fun unless you are able to add new treasures to your collection regularly. Keep your collection affordable. No bank loan officer will look sympathetically upon a request to borrow several hundred dollars for snow globes.

The good news is that if you do not have a great deal of time for the hunt, you can still actively collect snow globes. *Snow Biz* magazine is full of classified advertisements from individuals who sell, buy, and trade through the mail. Once you become part of the *Snow Biz* network, you will have regular buying opportunities. Another place to try advertising is in antiques and collectibles trade papers throughout the world, which run "seeker" advertising, i.e., classified advertisements from individuals seeking a specific group of objects. This form of advertising is very inexpensive – 20 to 35 cents per word. Also try flea market and collectibles show dealers, who are often willing to "pick" (keep a lookout for) snow globes for their better customers. In the highly competitive collecting atmosphere of the 1990s, it pays to have as many sets of eyes working for you as possible.

Of course, for those who love the hunt and have unlimited time,

ABOVE

A series of snow globes featuring girls in national costumes. Glass ball, Bakelite base, white snow. Decal label on base. Maker unknown. Late 1930s. 4⅛ in (10.5 cm) high.

there is no end to buying opportunities. Garage sales, community sales, white elephant tables at church bazaars, secondhand stores, and the recycling stores of charitable organizations such as the Salvation Army and Goodwill are worth checking on a regular basis. Antiques malls are frequently better hunting grounds than flea markets and antiques and collectibles shows. Once a snow globe works its way into the traditional collectible market, expect its price to rise as layers of profit are added to it by those involved in the selling and reselling process.

How available are the snow globes that you would like to collect? If you want to collect Atlas Crystal Works military-theme snow globes from the 1941–45 period, be prepared to be patient. Initially, you will add one or two a month to your collection. After a year, you will be lucky to add one every other month. On the other hand, if you collect snow globes from world capitals or one of the contemporary manufacturers such as Silvestri Corporation, you can add several snow globes a month to your collection for the next several decades.

When specializing, learn to venture outside the traditional snow globe markets and into the specialized collecting market of the crossover collectors. World's fair snow globes quickly work their way into the world's fair collecting market. These collectors have their own specialized newsletters and shows. You will have to pay the higher prices that these specialized markets command; but, you will add to your collection on a regular basis.

The most important aspect of any collecting philosophy is determining the categories in which you are going to collect. First, do not confine yourself to a single category. Snow globe collecting is too much fun to limit yourself this way. Second, select categories that include snow globes from outside your own country. Make every foreign trip a snow globe collecting expedition. Third, identify categories that are nostalgia driven, i.e., recapture favorite memories from the past. Disney, cartoon character, and snow globes manufactured during your teenage years are three possible approaches. Fourth, do not be afraid to change your mind. You will see more and more snow globes as you collect. Divorcing your first "love" is quite common in the collecting game. Finally, change your snow globes from inanimate to animate objects. Research your snow globes – the manufacturer, theme, and manner of marketing. Find out exactly when your favorite snow globes were made. Look for advertising and other paper ephemera with special meaning to your snow globe collection.

COLLECTING KEY #2 –
·········· BE AN AGGRESSIVE COLLECTOR ··········

Collecting is competitive; and, snow globe collecting is no exception. Collectors number in the hundreds. There are probably several in your neighborhood. Snow globe collecting is not a hobby that you are going to have to yourself.

While collecting competitiveness does not always take place on a friendly basis, it usually does within the snow globe collecting community. Established collectors willingly help new collectors get started. The motivation is not totally altruistic. They count on the new collector to become another set of eyes in their search for snow globes they need to complete their collection.

As quickly as possible, have a business card printed with your name, address, telephone number, and general wants. Distribute it generously. Place a business card advertisement in several trade periodicals. Answer responses promptly and courteously whether or not you are interested in buying. You want the person to keep looking. The payoff might not come until the third or fourth quote.

As soon as you feel comfortable, distribute a specific want list. Dealers, especially those who do not specialize in snow globes, are reluctant to pick when the want (topic) is too general. Bitter experience has taught them that, more often than not, the collector has the object that they have acquired and does not want a second example. However, their reaction is just the opposite to a specific list. They know the collector needs the object or it would not be on

THE COLLECTING COMMUNITY
· · · · · · · · · ·

Snow globe collectors love to visit and admire other collectors' treasures. Almost all are extremely gregarious – extroverts rather than introverts. It is not uncommon to find vacation routes planned to include a visit with another snow globe collector along the way. Implied in any visit is a willingness on the part of the visitors to host the visited at some future point. Finally, it should come as no surprise when the visitor arrives with a few snow globes for trading in his bag.

Friendship and hospitality are more important components in snow globe collecting than in most other collecting categories. Because snow globes are more affordable than many collectibles, collectors tend to buy any snow globe they can, whether they collect it or not. Then they trade it or sell it on at a modest profit.

The appearance of books, more and more snow globe articles in periodicals, and the inclusion of snow globe categories in collectibles price guides worry many established collectors. They are concerned that, as more and more people are attracted to snow globe collecting, prices will rise. Furthermore, individuals who are involved in collecting for profit rather than for love may be attracted to snow globes. As long as snow globe collectors refuse to buy globes at exorbitant prices and continue to emphasize friendship, hospitality, and trading as the collecting keys, snow globe collecting will remain a hobby rather than a business.

the list. Further, they know exactly what to seek.

There is one area where it does not pay to be aggressive – price. The one thing a snow globe collector does not need is a reputation for paying any amount to acquire a piece. Set firm price limits in your mind. You do not have to reveal them to dealers, just follow them. There is a thin line between aggressiveness and greed. Do not be a collector who crosses it.

COLLECTING KEY #3 –
······ PRACTICE PROPER CARE TECHNIQUES ·······

Snow globes are liquid-filled objects. In most cases that liquid is distilled water or water with chemical additives. No matter what the liquid is, snow globe collectors need to be concerned about three problems – clouding, evaporation, and freezing.

Snow globes survive best when they are kept in an environment with a humidity content of 50 to 60 percent, no temperature fluctuations, and a minimum exposure to light. For this reason, it is best not to store snow globes on shelves or in cabinets that are on the outside wall of a house or office, directly over or in line with heating air exchange ducts, or directly under or in line with a major light source.

This does not mean that you should keep your snow globes locked in a dark closet. It does mean that you must pay attention to storage. Keeping snow globes in the dark for long periods of time often results in water discoloring and turning brown. Collectors of holiday snow globes are well advised to leave their snow globes out year round rather than pack them away after each holiday.

Too much light from any source can damage a snow globe. Plastic snow globes left on windowsills quickly fade in color. Constant exposure to track, fluorescent, and even ordinary light bulbs can cause the same effect. It simply takes longer. In addition, light is a source of heat. Too much heat causes the colored backs of many plastic snow globes to flake. Once this happens, the snow globe is lost.

Consider rotating your snow globes once a month as a means of combating any environmental concerns. This is a good idea in any case. It is the perfect excuse to play with your collection.

Practice snow globe care the minute you purchase a snow globe. Collectors love to buy snow globes on their travels. Most simply wrap them and put them in a suitcase. Often, without considering the consequences, they place this suitcase in the trunk of a car or

ABOVE
Heat can cause the paint on the back of a plastic snow globe to deteriorate and flake off.

FIRE!
. . . . .

It is time to issue a snow globe fire hazard warning. One collector who displayed a series of ball-shaped snow globes on a low table near a window noticed that a black blemish appeared on the wooden base of some of his treasures. He discovered that his snow globes acted like a convex lens and focused the sunlight on a specific spot. If that light had struck a piece of paper or other flammable substance, a fire could easily have started. Never let sunlight strike your snow globes directly, especially those that are ball-shaped.

ABOVE
Hand-painted bisque figure of a cottage flanked by pine trees. Glass dome, brown glazed ceramic base, white snow. Maker unknown. Late 1930s. 4⅛ in (10.4 cm) high. (Restored.)

consign it to the baggage hold of an airplane. In the winter, car trunks and airplane storage areas are unheated. Likewise, they can overheat in the summer. No collector wants to open a suitcase and find the water in their new snow globe doing a slow boil. Many collectors have lost snow globes to freezing and cracking. Do not be one of them.

The answer is to carry a snow globe collecting handbag as part of your traveling gear. A flat-bottomed fabric bag with leather handles is ideal. A piece of foam in the bottom can act as a cushion. Your collecting handbag should also include tissue paper to wrap your purchases. Never allow a seller to wrap a snow globe in newspaper. If you want to know why, simply rub your fingers vigorously over a piece of newsprint with printing on it. Do not forget to wash your hands after this experiment.

Other items you might want to include in your handbag are copies of your snow globe collecting business card and want list, a copy of a list of the snow globes already in your collection, notebook and pencil to keep track of your purchases, and a camera for those snow globes priced above your means.

Carry your snow globe handbag with you. When flying, the pressurized cabin of the plane will prevent possible breakage. A heated or air-conditioned car avoids a sudden temperature change that can cause a snow globe to crack.

Many snow globe collectors sell, buy, and trade through the mail. Shipping presents problems. You never know how long a package will sit on a shipping dock or rest in an unheated transfer point. The postal service as well as most private carriers leave packages in a mail box or wrapped in plastic outside a door, often in inclement weather. Always ask the shipper to request a return receipt. This means that you have to sign for the package, and it is likely to remain in a semi-protected environment until you do. Tell the seller to avoid shipment during periods of extremely hot and cold weather.

Among the problems encountered by every collector are sellers who use price stickers or a marker pen to write on the surface of the snow globe to indicate the selling price. Removing the seller's sticker without leaving glue residue or the Magic Marker notation is not as easy as it sounds.

One of the best methods to remove glue residue from a price sticker is with a piece of sticky tape or masking tape. Strike the residue quickly with the tape. Often the second piece of tape will pick up the residue. Other substances that collectors have used include WD-40; Bestine, an art supply solvent and thinner; and Skin-so-Soft, a skin cream. One collector had success with De-Solv-It, a product sold at several chain drug stores in the U.S. Use a cotton swab and test all these products on the bottom of any plastic snow globe before using it on the visible surface. Never, never use an eraser – it just spreads the problem – or nail polish remover, which melts plastic.

First try to remove pen marks by gently rubbing with a crumpled tissue. If not successful, try soap and water. If still not successful, two other choices are Eucalyptus Oil (use the imported variety) and Grumbacher's Grumtine, available at art supply stores.

Collectors have tried a variety of substances to remove scratches on the surface of plastic snow globes. Products such as Flitz, Novus Plastic Polish #1 and #2, and 210 Plastic cleaner are reputed to make minor improvements. However, the product that collectors have found works best is tartar-control toothpaste. Apply it and rub gently. In some cases, it even removed marker-pen marks.

A cracked snow globe is a lost cause. Duco Cement and similar products can be used to repair cracked snow globes, but the repairs are painfully evident. Since snow globes are mass produced products, continuing your search for a snow globe in collectible condition makes more sense than living with one that has an all-too-visible repair.

Occasionally, it is necessary to clean your snow globes after purchase. Soap and water work best. In most cases, gentle rubbing with your hands will loosen the dirt. If you must use an abrasive surface, try a paper towel. Avoid any coarse material.

Likewise, be careful when dusting your snow globes. Use a light touch with a very soft dusting cloth. Better yet, use a feather duster. Dust particles can scratch a surface.

COLLECTING KEY #4
⋯ CREATIVELY DISPLAY YOUR SNOW GLOBES ⋯

Most collectors display their snow globes on wall or cabinet shelves. Several collectors have built lighted display cases designed specifically for their treasures. This display approach can encourage the line-them-up or pile-them-up technique: see how many snow globes you can cram into a limited space. More often than not, the individuality of each snow globe is lost.

NOTE

If the sticker is that of the retail merchant who sold the snow globe, consider the removal issue carefully. This sticker is part of the snow globe's history. It provides critical information on initial purchase price and retailer. Fortunately, most retail merchants placed their sales stickers on the bottom of the base.

ABOVE
Wooden stand made by Jay C. Sentz displays twelve snow globe ornaments. The set of snow globe ornaments contains eighteen snow globes in three sets of six. The sets are divided by their different bases (a chimney, a sack, and bows and garlands). "Wonders of Christmas" set made in Taiwan for the New England Collectors' Society. 1990. 3 in (7.6 cm) high.

Be creative in your display. First, organize your snow globes by themes. There is nothing wrong with a miscellaneous category for single globes and those that do not fit your main collecting themes. Second, break up the display approaches. Use a combination of shelves, cabinets, and table tops. Third, spend a few minutes looking at store-window displays. Note the use of pedestals, fabrics, and mirrored back drops. Try to be inventive.

Creating an attractive display does not have to be expensive. In order to achieve different viewing levels, buy some inexpensive stepped shelving designed for kitchen cabinet interiors. The plastic tops of spray cans are often bright, primary colors. Use them as pedestals for your snow globes. Small styrofoam and cardboard boxes, pill bottles, and inverted ashtrays also work well.

Ball-shaped globes are designed to be viewed from all angles. Your local hardware store sells self-adhesive mirror tiles. Place a row of these behind your snow globes to provide maximum viewing pleasure. In addition, your collection will appear to contain far more snow globes than it does.

Tilting a snow globe forward slightly can enhance its appearance when there is water loss. When snow globes are displayed above a person's visual plain, tilting the snow globes allows the information plaque to be read. Any number of objects, from coins to a portion of a sponge, can be used.

Every collector has one or more snow globes that are favored above all others. Do not hesitate to show them off. Consider using a small pinpoint spot light, a special color, or a framing method such as glass-covered dome on a stand or picture frame to call attention to them. These are your collection's best conversation pieces, the first snow globes that you want to talk about with anyone who looks at your collection.

One collector keeps a basket on the floor filled with her lesser globes. This approach creates a sense of discovery for anyone who chooses to handle them. The major drawback is the potential for surface scratching from careless handling.

COLLECTING KEY #5 –
CONSIDER CAREFULLY TAMPERING
············· WITH YOUR SNOW GLOBES ·············

What do you do with a snow globe in which the water has discolored or partially or totally evaporated, the snow has

A. Before restoration

B. After restoration

ABOVE
Hand-painted bisque figure of a boy with a dog. Glass dome, black ceramic base. The liquid had evaporated, leaving a brown mark along rim, and the white snow had turned tan with age. Atlas Crystal Works. Base contains patent information and Covington, TN. 1944–48. 4³/₁₆ in (10.5 cm) high.

clumped, or the base has chipped or been damaged? The collector's initial reaction is to restore it. In most cases, this approach is correct.

However, before replacing this or changing that, there are three points that need to be considered. First, how will the long-term collectibility of the snow globe be affected. As indicated previously, the jury is still out on this issue. If snow globe collecting follows the same trends as other collecting categories, it will eventually place a premium on a snow globe that is "period original." Second, how risky is the process? Some snow globes are difficult to open. Once liquid is replaced, the replacement liquid often tends to evaporate quicker than the original water. Mildewed snow cannot be cleaned; it can only be replaced. Third, do you have the expertise to perform the task at hand? At the moment, snow globe restoration is very much "amateur night." Individuals learn while they do. Unless restoration must be done immediately, it may pay to wait until restoration techniques are more fully developed in the future.

If darkness causes water to discolor, light will help restore it. One collector has discovered that putting an old glass snow globe with discolored water on a windowsill for an extended period of time causes the water to clear. Of course, in doing this, you risk the colors on the figurine or scenic panel fading.

A variety of substances were used to seal older snow globes in their ceramic and bakelite bases. Atlas Crystal Works used cement and tar. Other manufacturers used a plaster of Paris mixture. To replace the water and clean a dome, this substance has to be loosened. Soaking in water and using a picking device like a dental pick are the two commonly used methods. If successful, the globe can be twisted out from the base.

If an older snow globe has a decal, it is best not to do anything. Soaking the globe in water can destroy the decal. Coating the decal with shellac or another substance to prevent damage may in itself cause irreversible damage. Collectors have found that newer Austrian shiny plastic based snow globes and Italian shell-encrusted, snow globes are impossible to open.

If you are successful in removing the dome from the base, study it carefully. Remember, you have to put back together anything that you take apart. It is important to save every item. With the exception of the rubber washer, which can be replaced with modern equivalents, there are no replacement parts for the rest.

ABOVE
The rubber diaphragm of this snow globe has deteriorated, but the bisque figure is still secure in the glass container.

Pay particular attention to the metal or rubber closure piece. Collectors have tried cork and other substances as replacements, but none have proven totally satisfactory.

After you have removed the closure, once again study the construction carefully. Once you remove the figure and drain the water, everything tends to fall apart. Save the snow. Drain the water out over a piece of cheesecloth or a handkerchief. Carefully clean all the components.

Refilling the glass ball and reassembling is a learned skill. Try resting the ball upside down in a paper-lined glass. Fill it with water. Insert the figure and snow. Attach the closure piece. Check your handiwork. Chances are that the first several times you do this, you are going to find that you did not fill the globe adequately.

When reinserting the glass ball in the base, you need a seal. Do not use something permanent since you may have to repeat the process in a few years. American collectors have found that GE Silicone II, a clear caulking agent, works well.

Plastic dome-shaped snow globes present fewer problems. Most – but not all – have plugs that can be easily removed. Occasionally plugs have disintegrated or melted in the hole. Several globes from the 1950s have safety caps over the plugs. These can be carefully removed by sawing. When resealing, some collectors drip hot candle wax over the plug to strengthen the seal, especially if a different sized plug is used.

Most bottle-shaped globes cannot be opened. Some with applied figures have a flat panel covering the bottom, which can be removed by careful prying.

While tap water is usually adequate for refilling snow globes, collectors prefer distilled water. Snow globes made by Walter & Prediger have an interior coating that reacts with some tap water to cause tiny bubbles on the globe's interior surface.

The opening to fill plastic snow globes is often quite small. Among the suggestions for ease in filling are plastic hypodermic needles, holding it under a slowly running faucet, an icing tip used for frosting cakes, a perfume funnel, and a medicine dropper.

Collecting Key #6 –
············· Buy Extra Snow Globes ·············

You have already learned to buy duplicate snow globes and those of no interest to you for trading purposes. This key deals with "junkers," snow globes that have problems, but still have value.

ABOVE

A three-dimensional Santa in a cylindrical snow globe. Clear plastic cylinder, plastic white round base with knobs, white snow. Base marked "Made in Hong Kong." 1980s. 3³/₁₆ (8 cm) high.

At the moment, no one is manufacturing plugs for snow globes. It is highly unlikely that anyone will. Therefore, the principal source for replacement plugs is other snow globes. It may be worth ten cents to buy a globe that is cracked or deteriorating just to gain access to the spare plug. Furthermore, many different types of plug were used, and they are not universally interchangeable – the more spare plug varieties you have, the better.

You can buy commercial replacement snow, or use moth flakes as one collector does, but damaged snow globes are the best source for replacement snow. Cracking is the most commonly encountered problem, especially with plastic globes. The water has leaked out; but, the snow remains on the bottom. When you get really lucky, you can salvage the snow as well as a plug from a junker.

COLLECTING KEY #7 –
SUPPLEMENT YOUR COLLECTION
·········· WITH SNOW GLOBE EPHEMERA ··········

This category deals with objects on which an drawing or photograph of a snow globe appears on the surface. Impossible to find, you say. Hardly! Once you start looking for snow globe imagery, you will be amazed at how many pieces of snow globe ephemera you can find.

Two magazine covers that you will want for your collection are the December 1942 issue of *Good Housekeeping* and the January 1970 issue of *Jack and Jill*. Bumper stickers, calendars, greeting cards, magazine advertisements, newspaper cartoons, notecards, posters, shopping bags, and T-Shirts are just a few of the places that you will find snow globes portrayed.

Included in this category are broadsides, catalogs, and other forms of sales literature from snow globe manufacturers and distributors. Early examples are difficult to find. Readily available are the giftware catalogs of present-day distributors such as Kurt Adler, Enesco, and Silvestri. Acquire copies and save them. In twenty years, they will be important dating and research documents.

COLLECTING KEY #8 –
·········· KEEP PRICE IN PERSPECTIVE ··········

What is a snow globe worth? While sellers try to convince you that it is the price that they are asking, the simple truth is that you must

ABOVE
Book jacket for *Babe Ruth Caught in a Snowstorm* by John Alexander Graham, published by Houghton-Mifflin, copyright 1973. 6 in × 8 in (15.25 × 20.3 cm).

TOP
Book jacket for *Whiteout: Lost in Aspen* by Ted Conover, published by Random House, 1991. 6½ in × 9½ in (16.5 × 24 cm). Model of the snow globe was made by Manhattan Model Shop.

ABOVE
Identical zoo souvenir snow globes from three locations.

decide what any snow globe is worth to you. Forget book prices. Price guides are only that, a guide. The question that you need to ask yourself is: What is this snow globe worth to me?

Experienced collectors have disciplined themselves to ask this question before even picking up a snow globe for inspection at an antiques mall or shop, flea market, or collectors' fair. When the price marked on the snow globe is so high that it is beyond negotiating range, they walk away. Walking away, especially if it is a snow globe you want badly, is very hard to do.

Remember that snow globes are mass produced. Each example was manufactured in the thousands. Many had production runs that lasted longer than a decade. Concepts such as rare, one-of-a-kind, etc., have no meaning.

The mass production aspect of snow globes means that it pays to shop around. If condition does not match your standards, walk away. If the price is prohibitive, refuse to pay it. Learn and practice patience.

One of the mistakes novice collectors make is overpaying for commonly found snow globes. It takes several years of experience to learn to differentiate between commonly seen snow globes and those which are more difficult to find. Refrain from buying expensive snow globes until you fully understand the market.

COLLECTING KEY #9 – ·········· COLLECT FOR THE LONG TERM ··········

It is not easy to sustain collecting enthusiasm. While nostalgia and the fun of collecting attracts a collector to a collecting category, it is findability and affordability that keeps the collector's enthusiasm at a fever pitch. The key is to avoid collector burnout.

Novice collectors are generally so enthusiastic that they can hardly restrain themselves from buying. Once they have assembled their basic core collection, they slow down as it becomes harder and harder and more and more expensive to find the snow globes they want. If only it was the other way around, start slow and finish with flourish.

New collectors are wise to start slowly. This stretches the collecting process and makes the fun last longer. One method to achieve this goal is to make certain that initial purchases are only of snow globes in excellent to mint condition. Any commonly found snow globe acquired for the collector's collection should look as though it just came off the assembly line.

Carefully study the figurines and scenic panels. Buy only snow globes whose central images have pizzazz. Most figurines and scenic panels were and still are hand-painted. This means that you will encounter slight differences in the same dome. Look for painting that is well done and aesthetically pleasing.

If you are confused, acquire three identical snow globes and place them side by side. Study them until you notice the subtle differences between them. Determine which one appears the best to you and then ask yourself why. There is no reason why the eye of the connoisseur should not work as well with snow globes as it does with fine art.

COLLECTING KEY #10 – SHARE YOUR COLLECTION AND KNOWLEDGE

There is no fun being a closet snow globe collector. Get your collection out in the open and display it. A true collector never apologizes for what he or she collects. The joy is in the act of collecting, not in what is collected.

Displaying your snow globe collection is the best publicity you can achieve. Before you know it, individuals will start contributing to your collection. Make certain that you follow one simple rule – be honest about how the gift fits into your collection. Is the snow globe one you are likely to keep or trade? When it is the latter, put a positive slant on the gift by thanking the individual and telling them that they have made it possible for you to trade for a snow globe that has long eluded you.

Snow globe collectors share their collections with each other. It is customary. If you do not want to share, then do not join the collectors' club and attend meetings. Courtesy requires advance notice of any visit and the right to decline a visit if the timing is inconvenient. A visit by another collector allows you to talk shop. A visit from another collector is always welcome.

Share not only your collection, but your research knowledge as well. No one expects you to share your buying sources. A smart collector keeps these confidential. You can share information about new snow globes that you have seen, historical research you may have uncovered, and your enthusiasm.

ABOVE
A clear plastic bottle-shaped snow globe, viewed sideways. Back of bottle painted dark blue, white snow. Bottom of bottle plastic panel marked "Made in Hong Kong." 1960s. 5⅛ in (13 cm) long. 2⅜ in (6 cm) high.

SNOW GLOBE
MANUFACTURERS

Snow globes researchers have been able to identify a number of the leading manufacturers and distributors of snow globes in America, Austria, France, and Germany. Given the large number of unattributed globes, this research has probably only scratched the surface, especially identifying manufacturing sources in the Far East, sources that distributors prefer to keep to themselves. Other countries to which the manufacture of snow globes has been attributed are Belgium, Bulgaria, Great Britain, Italy, and Russia.

Nancy McMichael was the first to call attention to the fact that cultural preferences can be used at least to identify the country of origin of some snow globes. For example, Italian pieces are often identified by their bright primary colors, unrealistic scenic panels, and exterior figurines, and the bases, which are elongated (some have free-standing flats of buildings), fluted, or scalloped with seashells or colored stones attached. Be careful attributing country of origin to snow globes with foreign language panels; many were made by outside manufacturers.

The following information about manufacturers and distributors comes from a variety of printed sources with additional data supplied by current mass market manufacturers and distributors.

·················· AMERICA ··················

Kurt S. Adler, Inc., New York, New York. Kurt S. Adler established Kurt S. Adler/Santa's World more than forty years ago. Today the company is the country's largest importer, designer, and supplier of Christmas ornaments, decorations, and accessories, with products from over 200 factories in more than 30 nations across the globe, including China, Germany, Hong Kong, Japan, Mexico, Philippines, Sri Lanka, Taiwan, and other nations in Europe and South America.

Among its many accomplishments is its innovative design team. Assisting Kurt S. Adler in the decision-making process are Clifford and Howard, two of his sons. In addition to the company headquarters in New York, Kurt S. Adler/Santa's World has eighteen showrooms throughout the United States.

Atlas Crystal Works, Trenton, New Jersey and Covington, Tennessee. William M. Snyder, an attorney, built a glass container factory in Jackson, Mississippi, during the Depression. In 1939 Snyder sold his glass container factory to the Knox Glass Bottling Company and moved his family to Canada. In 1941 Snyder and his family moved to Washington, D.C., where Snyder was involved in litigation with Knox, and he set up a sidewalk souvenir stall

LEFT
Cube snow globe with clear plastic sides. Three hand-painted injection-molded units. Trees and a mountain are painted on the back panel. Molded figure on top. White snow. Base marked "Kurt Adler, Inc . . .." 1980s. 4 in (10 cm) high.

RIGHT **Glass dome, black glazed ceramic base, white snow. Atlas Crystal Works, Trenton, base. 1941–43. 4⅛ in (10.5 cm) high. (Restored).**

opposite the United States Capitol. One of the most popular items he sold was an imported Japanese "snowfall" paperweight of the Washington Monument.

Three key elements occurred at the end of 1941 that resulted in William M. Snyder becoming one of America's leading manufacturers of snow globes during the 1940s. As 1941 progressed, the supply of snow globes from Japan became uncertain. Snyder's litigation then ended favorably, making finance available to start a new business venture. On December 7, 1941, the Japanese bombed Pearl Harbor, and America declared war on Japan. There would be no more snow globes from Japan for the foreseeable future.

As the war progressed, more and more Trenton ceramic plants were redirected to produce material for the war effort. While Snyder's supply of glass bottle containers remained steady, he encountered increased difficulties in ensuring his supply of bisque figures and ceramic bases.

Complicating matters further were the harsh Trenton winters, when it was not unusual for snow globes to freeze and crack in transit. To help eliminate this problem, Snyder installed a rubber diaphragm in the base so the water could expand and contract without damaging the globe. This also prevented bubbles from appearing in the water, another manufacturing problem.

As 1943 ended, the company faced a supply crisis. The only answer was to move. A former soft-drink bottling plant in Covington, Tennessee, was for sale, and after a brief courtship, Snyder moved his operations there.

Upon arriving in Covington, Snyder installed his own kiln to make the bisque figures and ceramic bases. The bisque figures were cast. Initially bases were jiggered. Eventually a hydraulic press was acquired to speed up the process and Atlas continued manufacturing throughout the year.

Bill Snyder also became more active. He and William, Sr. continued to be the principal snowmakers, performing their magic at night after the employees left. The snow globe snow, its formula a carefully guarded industrial secret, was made by melting large blocks of paraffin wax in a pot, adding camphor flakes, stirring, and pouring the resulting mixture onto cookie sheets. After the mixture cooled, it was broken into chunks. Water was added to it and then ground into flakes in an old meat grinder.

Atlas Crystal Works snow globes were sold three ways: through wholesale distributors to the gift shop trade, retailers, and military contracts. The suggested retail price for a snow globe was $1.00. Wholesale distributors were charged $4.80 per dozen; retailers paid $6.00 per dozen. Two of the wholesale giftware distributors that purchased Atlas Crystal Works snow globes were Goldfarb and Star. The company also supplied overseas sources.

Snow globes from Atlas were extremely popular during the war. Snyder could not produce them fast enough. Civilian as well as military themes were utilized, and over a hundred different motifs were eventually produced. By the end of the war, most families owned several of these novelties.

By 1946 the snow globe market was saturated, and snow globes became a very hard sell. As consumer goods multiplied, there was increased competition for the buyer's attention. Snow globes were not a high priority purchase, and the cost of raw materials rose significantly. The company continued to promote its product through sale sheets, catalogs, and color post cards. "Bill" Snyder spent the summer of 1948 traveling the country soliciting orders.

Eventually William Snyder accepted the inevitable. By the late 1940s the kiln that had fired figures and bases was used to make souvenir plates, a product for which the company has since become internationally renowned. Atlas Crystal Works survives today through its holding, World Wide Art Studios.

A series of disastrous floods in Covington destroyed all the records of the snow globe

ABOVE
Workers at the Atlas Crystal Works in 1946. With no previous art training, these women hand painted 1000 figures a day.

manufacturing period. The company no longer has copies of its advertising sheets, catalogs, promotional post cards, or sales records. Its early logo – Atlas holding up a snow globe world paperweight – was changed to avoid confusion with the products of Atlas China when the company switched its main output to souvenir plates.

Preservation of the Atlas Crystal Works snow globe legacy now rests in the hands of snow globe collectors.

[Note: Special thanks to William "Bill" Snyder, Jr., son of William M. Snyder, for providing this information.]

ABOVE
**Salt and pepper shaker.
Rectangular plastic imitation TV
set with snow scene. Snow globe
has a hand-painted injection-
molded panel of birds. Silver
glitter, footed. Top panel slides
left or right for salt or pepper.
Base marked "Made in Hong
Kong/NO. T 3578." 1960s. 4 in
(10 cm) wide, 2¾ in (7 cm) high.**

Driss Company, Chicago, Illinois, Driss created snow globes that capitalized on popular songs (Frosty the Snowman and Rudolph the Red Nosed Reindeer) and television programs (Davy Crockett and The Lone Ranger) of the late 1950s. Central figurines were injection-molded and hand-painted.

Enesco, Elk Grove Village, Illinois. In 1958 Enesco was created as a division of N. Shure Company, Chicago. Following the sale of the parent company, the small import division reorganized as Enesco, formed from the phonic initials of the original company name – N.S. Co. Eugene Freedman as president and chief executive officer provided the leadership to make Enesco one of the most respected names in the giftware industry. Today Enesco is the cornerstone of Enesco Worldwide Giftware Group, with subsidiaries in Canada, Great Britain, Germany, Australia, and Hong Kong, as well as product-producing businesses in the United States.

Enesco moved to its international headquarters to Elk Grove Village, Illinois, in 1984. The Enesco name is known to a host of collectors, ranging from those who collect Precious Moments to The Memories of Yesterday Collection based on the work of the British artist Mabel Lucie Attwell. Enesco's licensed giftware includes the work of artists such as Jim Davis (GARFIELD), Walt Disney, and Lesley Anne Ivory (Ivory Cats). Currently Enesco is a wholly owned subsidiary of Stanhome, Inc., Westfield, Massachusetts.

Louis Marx Company. Louis Marx (1896–1982) began his toy career working for Ferdinard Strauss, "The Toy King." After a dispute with Strauss, Louis Marx and his brother began to manufacture their own line of toys in 1921. By the 1950s Louis Marx was the largest manufacturer of toys in the world. The company owned six plants in the United States and an interest in plants in seven foreign countries. In April 1972 Marx sold his company to the Quaker Oats Company, who in turn sold it in 1976 to Dunbee-Combex-Marx, Europe's largest toy manufacturer. Marx entered bankruptcy in 1980. In 1982 American Plastics bought many of the Marx assets, including their production molds, and began issuing restrikes from the original molds in 1990.

Marx entered the snow globe market in the mid-1960s introducing a number of six dome sets ranging from snow globes with a Christmas scene to those picturing motifs from the American West. The plastic oval-based, dome-shaped snow globes featured well-painted injection-molded central figures and an abundance of snow.

Progressive Products, Union, New Jersey. In the 1950s this company produced ball-shaped snow globes that rested on a sloping, flat, rectangular base. Although the company produced souvenir and stock theme snow globes, it is best known among collectors for snow globes that were advertising giveaways, commemorated a special event, or served as incentive and other special rewards. The company used oil instead of water to fill their globes.

B. Shackman Company, New York, New York. A major importer of snow globes into the United States beginning in the 1930s and extending into the post-war period. Many of the company's early imports were German snow globes manufactured by Koziol, but by the 1950s the company's principal source of snow globes was Hong Kong. Prior to World War II, the company also bought American-made snow globes from Modern Novelty Manufacturing Company.

Shackman's initial snow globe imports focused on generic and Christmas motifs. In the 1970s the company introduced snow globes for other holidays such as Valentine's Day, Easter, and Halloween.

Silvestri Corp., Chicago, Illinois. Silvestri Corporation is a leading importer and wholesale distributor of Christmas decorations, seasonal holiday gifts, and decorative home accessories. The company began in 1940 as Silvestri Art Manufacturing Company specializing in plaster vases, plaques, statues, pedestals, and similar articles. George Silvestri and Bernard J. Gorman, two company salesmen, purchased the company from Geroge's uncle. An early company success story was the introduction of miniature Christmas tree lights in the 1950s.

George Silvestri sold the company in 1965 to a corporation which adopted the name Silvestri Corporaion in 1969. In addition to seven major United States showrooms, the company has offices and warehouse in Hong Kong, the Philipnes, and Taiwn. Silvestri also imports goods from the People's Republic of China, India, Korea, Thailand, and several European countries.

·················· AUSTRIA ··················

Erwin Perzy, Vienna, Austria. Erwin Perzy founded the company in the early 1900s. Its earliest snow globes had a religious theme and a trademark black base.

In the 1950s the company introduced some secular motifs and scored a major success at the Nuremburg Fair with a snowman motif snow globe. Perzy then began supplying large American department stores with snow globes.

The company has always stressed quality and takes pride in the fact that its snow takes approximately two minutes to fall — the formula is a closely guarded secret.

Perzy also manufactures limited edition snow globes. One of the most sought after is the Republican party's elephant snow globe produced during the Reagan presidency.

Perzy currently offers 50 different snow globe motifs and Erwin Perzy III continues to seek innovation in motif and construction; he aims one day to create a completely round globe without a base.

ABOVE
Winged angel holding a pine tree. Glass ball, plastic pedestal base, white snow. Base marked "Made in Austria," Erwin Perzy. No date. 4½ in (11.4 cm) high.

ABOVE
Two hand-painted, injection-molded panels (Eiffel Tower in a circle, and a domed light blue background panel). Clear plastic dome and white oval-footed base, white snow. Base marked "MADE IN FRANCE." 1990s. 2½ in (6.3 cm). Dome has a top plug.

················· FRANCE ·················

Ets C & Cie. A company active in the manufacture of snow globes for a brief time in the post-war period. Its snow globes were egg-shaped and rested on a square base made of glass on plastic.

Paul Viandel. Viandel was the major manufacturer of French souvenir and religious snow globes. Viandel preferred a blue-toned plastic instead of the more traditional clear plastic for the domed container. The plug was located on the top of the globe, a feature associated with Sieper snow globes from Germany.

················· GERMANY ·················

Koziol Geschenkartikel GmbH, Erbach/Odenwald. Koziol first presented its snow globes at the Frankfurter Messe in 1948. There were two varieties: round base, bullet-shaped globes, used for the religious assortment, and oval-based, steep-sided domes for the rest of the line.

In 1951, Koziol introduced the *Traumkugel* (dream globe) with a highly romantic theme.

Koziol continued to add new products to its line and after 35 years of producing traditionally shaped globes, it introduced its first large-format snow globe in 1984.

Koziol's licensing program, especially with Disney, has helped revive worldwide interest in snow globes, as did the jumbo-sized snow globe launched in 1986, and the Koziol version of the largest snoiw globe ever, produced in 1987.

Richard Sieper and Son. A German manufacturer active in the early 1950s. Their early snow globes had a snowflake plug at the top. It was eventually replaced with a flower plug.

Walter & Prediger, Kaufbeuren. Hans Walter founded this company in 1947. He introduced the oval-based, dome-shaped plastic snow globe. A major manufacturer of plastic snow globes, Walter & Prediger are known for their traditional scenic motifs ranging from folk tales to mountain landscapes. To date, over 3,000 different images have appeared in their snow globes.

ABOVE
Nativity Scene. Clear plastic tapered conical shape and white oval base, white snow. White plastic cap over top fill hole. Plastic rays extend down from the middle of the cap. Base marked "Ges. Geschutz/Made in Germany." Attributed to Koziol. Early 1950s. 3 in (7.6 cm) high.

INDEX

ACKNOWLEDGEMENTS

Our deepest appreciation to the following individuals who provided research information used in this book: Joan Anderson, Division of Science and Technology, Carnegie Library of Pittsburgh; Robert Ayen, Assistant Product Developer, Giftware, Silvestri Corp.; Mrs. Chabrel, French Trade Office, New York; Carolyn Cobb and Gail Moody, Neiman Marcus; Jimmie Corder, Personnel Director, World Wide Art Studios; Ron Kaiser, FanDome; Stephan Koziol, Koziol Geschenkartikel GmbH; Ms. Patti Glaser-Martin, John Michael Kohler Art Center; Nancy McMichael; Erwin Perzy III, Erwin Perzy; Christopher Pica; Pat Shaw, Senior Director of Communications, Enesco; William "Bill" M. Snyder, Jr.; Jan Smith, Curator, Bergstrom-Mahler Museum; Mrs. Tomko, Pennsylvania Room, Carnegie Library of Pittsburgh; and, Hans Walter, Walter & Prediger.

The snow globes illustrted in this book come from the collections of Bergstrom-Mahler Museum, Miriam Beim, John Michael Kohler Art Center, Connie A. Moore, Harry L. Rinker, Herbert Rolfes, Gloria M. and Jay C. Sentz, and Susan Whitenack. Thank you for sharing your treasures with our readers. Harry L. Rinker, Jr., did the photography. FanDomes, a division of the Kintra Group, Koziol Geschenkartikel GmbH, Erwin Perzy, and World Wide Art Studios supplied illustration material.

Finally, thank you to Stephen Paul and Katie Preston of Quintet Publishing Ltd. for their patience, persistence, and help in the creation of this book. The authors remain deeply in their debt.